Collecting national park stamps The Levering Family, Ohio • **Collecting pine cones in the woods** The Vermans, New York • **Collecting seashells on the beach** The Fletcher Family, California • **Collecting to create acorn dolls** The Colvins, California • **Collecting trash on nature hikes** The Myers Family, Illinois • **Cooking over an open fire** The Torgersen Family, Sweden • **Crawdad catching in our creek** The Johnson Family, North Carolina • **Creating artwork from nature items** The Hayes Family, Alabama • **Creating in the mud kitchen** The Iveys, Tennessee • **Creating mud pie masterpieces** The Gunther Gang, Utah • **Creating nature color palettes** Carryduff Playgroup, Northern Ireland • **Cross-country skiing and skijoring** The Gifford Family, Alaska • **Crunching through the autumn leaves** The Abwat-Johnson Family, Warwickshire, England • **Cultivating our backyard garden** The Hayes Family, Florida • **Cutting, splitting, and stacking wood** The Loucks Family, Minnesota • **Dam building in the lochs** The Dickinsons, Scotland • **Dance parties in the backyard** The Lewis Family, Texas • **Dancing on mountain summits** The O'Mahony Family, Virginia • **Dancing under a full moon** The McKenna Family, Iowa • **Dark pajama walk with glowsticks** The Moyer Family, Ohio • **Decorating a night tree together** The Harmon Family, New York • **Decorating trees with edible ornaments** The DePue Family, New York • **Digging clay from the creek** The Zachowski Family, Ohio • **Digging holes in the backyard** The Hodges, South Carolina • **Discussing books read on horseback** The Smith Family, Louisiana • **Downhill skiing in Idaho** The Garbers, Idaho • **Drawing chalk houses on the driveway** The Thorlakson Family, Washington • **Early evening headlamp "dark walks"** The Allen Family, Maine • **Eating breakfast on the porch** The Kileys, Pennsylvania • **Egg hunt in the forest** The Kohler-Karpouzis, Germany • **Exploration walk through town** The Hamptons, Georgia • **Exploring all of Rhode Island** The Knolls, Rhode Island • **Exploring and finding leaves in the woods** The Marquez Family, Mexico • **Exploring different zoos nationwide** The Emmolo Family, New Jersey • **Exploring local historical landscapes** The Marks Family, New York • **Exploring our neighborhood retention pond** The Gould Family, Illinois • **Exploring a brand-new trail** The Yates Family, Maine • **Exploring and experiencing different countries** The Lowrie Family, Florida • **Exploring castle ruins** The Currans, Northern Ireland • **Exploring mudflats in Maine** The Highbaugh Family, Kentucky • **Exploring national par**... Moradi Family, Michigan • **Exploring North Shore tide pools** The Jacoby Family, Hawaii • **Exploring our grandparents' woods** The Ritger Fernandez Family, Wisc... **playgrounds within sixty miles** The Clark Kids, Ohio • **Exploring state and national parks** The Smith Tribe, Montana • **Exploring the Pacific Ocean together** ... Hawaii • **Exploring tide pools and driftwood** The Vetetoe Family, Florida • **Fairy hikes in the forest** The Katz Gologor Family, New York • **Falconry with red-tailed ha**... Family, Wisconsin • **Falconry, walking, and exploring** The Eadie Family, England • **Family picnic at a park** The Monroe-West Family, Tennessee • **Farm work with**... Family, Michigan • **Feeding and caring for livestock** The Siddall Family, Michigan • **Feeding the birds at Kensington** The Hirzel Family, Wisconsin • **Filling pocke**... **treasures** The Chings, Yorkshire, England • **Finding bugs in the garden** The Grimes, California • **Finding a perfect climbing tree** The Dehline Burt Family, Montana • **Finding hea**... **rocks** The Thulls, Kansas • **Finding bug friends outside** The Ryberg Family, Texas • **Finding daily moments of beauty** The Woods Family, New Brunswick, Canada • **Finding shark teeth on the beach** The Qualls Family, Ma... **everywhere** The Myers Clan, Illinois • **Finding new waterfalls** The Otto Family, Missouri • **Fishing at sunset** Alden & Zavier Peterson (& Their Parents), Virginia • **Flashlight hide-and-seek** The Stunkel... **surprise creeks on hikes** The Kasperik Family, California • **Floating freshwater springs in Florida** The Orwigs, Florida • **Floating on the lake** The Quagl... **Flashlight hike and flashlight tag** The Kasperik Family, California • **Flying feelings in strong winds** Mummy, Daddy & Albert, England • **Following a trail of an**... York • **Flower suncatchers are our favorite** The Weiss Family, Missouri • **Forest fairy tea party** The Moniz-Montano Ohana, Hawaii • **Forest fort building with family** Tr... California • **Footraces in the grass** The Sanderson Family, Illinois • **Forest fairy tea party** The Moniz-Montano Ohana, Hawaii • **Forest walk to hammock hangout** The Viviano Family, Tennessee • **Forest**... Maryland • **Forest school fun with toddlers** The Parkin Family, County Durham, England • **Forest walk with horses** Victoria and Laura, Germany • **Front yard soccer with dad** The Suchanek Family, Missouri • **Full n**... **out mushrooms** The Sluises, Maine • **Forest walks with horses** Victoria and Laura, Germany • **Front yard soccer with dad** The Suchanek Family, Missouri • **Full n**...

The Somarriba Family, Texas • **Full moon family walks** The Andress Family, Oregon • **Full moon hikes with treats** The Jurado Family, Air Force family—home is where the heart is • **Gaga ball and beach days** The Berens Family, Ohio • **Gazing at the bright stars** The Lanier Family, Ohio • **Giant field ice-puddle sliding** The Wiebe Family, Ontario, Canada • **Giving our toys a bath** The Dees Family, Alabama • **Going to the zoo** The Van Oost-Lenaerts Family, Belgium • **Going camping for the weekend** The Bonnes Family, Georgia • **Going down a mud slide** The Hill-Davis Family, Cheshire, England • **Going for family bike rides** The Brownfield Family, North Carolina • **Going for morning walks** The Ruggles Family, Florida • **Mushroom foraging in fall** The Moore Family, Ohio • **Going on a caterpillar hunt** The Nix Family, Indiana • **Grilling hotdogs over an open fire** The Horwood Eriksson Family, Sweden • **Growing food and eating it** The Farrell Family, Suffolk, England • **Growing a garden** The Peters Family, Mississippi • **Growing veggies from seed** The Merkel Family, Victoria, Australia • **Hammock swinging** The Aylmer Family, Maine • **Hand-feeding chickadees** The Rodenburg Family, Ontario, Canada • **Happy family backyard camping** The Shaifuls Family, Malaysia • **Harvesting fall vegetables** The Schultz Family, Oklahoma • **Harvesting pawpaw fruit in September** The Dydas, Maryland • **Harvesting wine grapes in the fall** The Kuehns, Pennsylvania • **Headlamp nighttime sledding** The Bower Crew, Michigan • **Hide-and-seek in the woods** The Barker-Noels, England • **Hiking at Karura Forest** The Ndagjjimana Family, Nairobi, Kenya • **Hiking along a frozen river** The Sisson Family, Arizona • **Hiking an unknown trail** The Kerr Family, British Columbia, Canada • **Hiking at Turkey Run** Team Hull, Illinois • **Hiking barefoot in the woods** The Grau Family, Florida • **Hiking Hocking Hills State Park** The Fowler Family, Ohio • **Hiking in Acadia National Park** The Johnson Family, Maine • **Hiking in costumes year round** The Betheas, South Carolina • **Hiking in Ludington State Park** The Walker Family, Michigan • **Hiking in the great outdoors** The Kinkead Family, Ohio • **Hiking in the rainforest rain** The Snyder Family, Hawaii • **Hiking on the Appalachian Trail** The Wolf Family, Connecticut • **Hiking our state parks** The Cline Family, Indiana • **Hiking scavenger hunts** The Mullins Girls, Alabama • **Hiking the Appalachian Trail** The Paolino Family, Pennsylvania • **Hiking the Bruce Trail** The St. Amand Family, Ontario, Canada • **Hiking the Shirley Canyon Trail** The Alves Jensen Family, Oregon • **Hiking to a frozen waterfall** The Judd Family, Utah • **Hiking to reach a summit** The Ernst Family, Michigan • **Hiking with our homeschool group** The Hoffmans, Virginia • **Hiking with our nature journals** The Herman Family, Florida • **Hiking Zion National Park** The Dodds Family, Utah • **Hot chocolate at the beach** The Kelleher-Bennett Family, Northumberland, England • **Hot chocolate hikes in winter** The Chersida Girls, Germany • **Hot tub in a blizzard** The Taylor/Anning Family, Nova Scotia, Canada • **Hot tub totes in the snow** The Orkins, Maine • **Hunting for hearts in nature** The Dollarhide Family, Texas • **Hunting for Sasquatch** The Lancasters, Nebraska • **Hunting for sharks' teeth** The Gishler Family, Florida • **Hunting morels in the spring** The Heleski Family, Michigan • **Ice cream on the porch** The Holland Family, North Carolina • **Ice-painting in the summer** The Vickerys, Florida • **Ice-skating around our swamp** The Bernards, Maine • **Ice-skating on Ghost Lake** The Kutama Family, Alberta, Canada • **Ice-skating rink in backyard** The McClouds, Michigan • **Icy puddle crunching** The Burns Family, Oregon • **Identifying and foraging for mushrooms** The Wolfe Family, Pennsylvania • **Identifying plants and insects** The Grays, Vermont • **Identifying plants on nature walks** The Stone Family, Nevada • **Insect hunting, identifying, and releasing** Family Adam-Haezebrouck, Ghana • **Journaling our nature discoveries** The Murchie Family, Texas • **Jumping into leaf piles** The Falls Family, Missouri • **Jumping in leaf piles** The Gordon Family, Virginia • **Jumping in mud and puddles** The Cropleys, West Sussex, England • **Jumping off the Black Rocks** The Machtemes Family, Michigan • **Kickball along an abandoned dirt road** The Westons, California • **Laser tag in the woods** The Cannon Family, British Columbia, Canada • **Lying in the grass** The Parkers, Florida • **Leaf and flower petal art** The Edgerles, Wisconsin • **Leaf rubbing in fall** The Findley Family, Virginia • **Leaping across the salty surf** The Muffs, California • **Letterboxing in the woods** The Fabers, Michigan • **Life in the sandbox** The Robinsons, Ontario, Canada • **Listening to the wind in the trees** The Van Dijk-Moghaddam Family, The Netherlands • **Log-hopping across vernal pools** The Boothroyd Family, Michigan • **Long beach day with friends** The Shafer Family, Michigan • **Long days at the beach** The Celmo Family, California • **Looking for four-leaf clovers** The Uzumecki/Strack Family, Illinois • **Looking for beach glass** The Klimczuk Family, Michigan • **Looking for the full moon** The McGeever Family, Scotland • **Looking up at the moon** The Merolles, South Carolina •

relationships in the great outdoors. I've never felt more motivated to be present, free, and unabashedly me."

Amber O'Neal Johnston, author of *A Place to Belong*

"A timely book! Ginny expertly captures the attention of her audience with humor and candid stories, taking us all deeper into the importance of play and authentic connection with others. There is much truth in *Until the Streetlights Come On*."

Angela Hanscom, author of *Balanced and Barefoot*

"Ginny is a special person who has written a very special book. *Until the Streetlights Come On* does not hanker for the past but instead looks ahead to the time where increasingly children will need to be self-motivated, adaptable, creative problem solvers and team builders. She skillfully lays out a way that will feel in flow with everyday life, giving space for children to have a childhood and deeply play. In simple and joyful terms, Ginny has described a pathway to giving our children a childhood so that they can grow into successful, competent, and confident adults. She has done it with a warmth that leaves us with the feeling 'I can do this.'"

Kim John Payne, MEd, author of *Emotionally Resilient Tweens and Teens*, *Simplicity Parenting*, *The Soul of Discipline*, and *Beyond Winning*

"*Until the Streetlights Come On* takes us back to the cul-de-sacs and customs of our youth when play was more than just a pastime, it was a rite of passage. Rousing and replete with research, this book is a primer for preserving play and giving childhood back to its rightful owners—our kids."

Ainsley Arment, founder of Wild + Free

"Call it what you like: play, adventure, or preparing kids to save the world. Connecting with nature is fun, healthy, and vitally important."

Alastair Humphreys, author of *Microadventures* and a National Geographic Adventurer of the Year

"For every swirling emotion you and your kids are navigating right now—*Underwhelmed! Overwhelmed! Everything in between!*—play promises hope and connection on the other side. And in her brilliantly illuminating book, Ginny Yurich is the guide who leads you straight there and beyond. Overflowing with reflective prompts and practical ideas for deeper play, *Until the Streetlights Come On* is the definitive guide to play for those of us who can't remember what it means to play—and for those of us who can't afford to forget."

Erin Loechner, author and founder of Other Goose

"I had planned to read one chapter of *Until the Streetlights Come On* daily until I completed it, but once I opened it, I finished the entire book because I couldn't stop reading. In each chapter, I felt seen, challenged, and inspired to fiercely protect my family's slow margin. Ginny offers a special balance of science, heart, and soul as she presents a master class for prioritizing play, honoring childhood, and building

Until the Streetlights Come On

Until THE Streetlights Come On

HOW A RETURN TO PLAY BRIGHTENS OUR PRESENT AND PREPARES KIDS FOR AN UNCERTAIN FUTURE

GINNY YURICH, MEd

BakerBooks

a division of Baker Publishing Group
Grand Rapids, Michigan

© 2023 by Virginia Yurich

Published by Baker Books
a division of Baker Publishing Group
Grand Rapids, Michigan
BakerBooks.com

Printed in the United States of America

Library of Congress Cataloging-in-Publication Data
Names: Yurich, Ginny, author.
Title: Until the streetlights come on : how a return to play brightens our present and
    prepares kids for an uncertain future / Ginny Yurich
Description: Grand Rapids, Michigan : Baker Books, a division of Baker Publishing
    Group, 2023. | Includes bibliographical references.
Identifiers: LCCN 2023008915 | ISBN 9781540903402 (cloth) | ISBN 9781493443383
    (ebook)
Subjects: LCSH: Play—Psychological aspects. | Play—Social aspects. | Children—
    Mental health. | Physical fitness for children.
Classification: LCC BF717 .Y87 2023 | DDC 155.4/18—dc23/eng/20230412
LC record available at https://lccn.loc.gov/2023008915

The author is represented by Alive Literary Agency, www.aliveliterary.com.

Baker Publishing Group publications use paper produced from sustainable forestry practices and post-consumer waste whenever possible.

23 24 25 26 27 28 29   7 6 5 4 3 2 1

To my family.
I delight in each and every one of you.
To Jackson, Vivian, Charlie, Brooklyn, and Winnie Jo.
You were each made for a purpose, and it is my deepest honor
to have a front-row seat in watching your purpose play out.

To Josh.
There is absolutely no way I could've
done this without you. Thank you.
Someday I will move the stacks and stacks of books.

To Keilah.
Sorry I forgot you last time. You're a favorite part
of my life, and you have been since we first met.

To Erin.
Your words made me a writer, and I'm forever grateful.

Contents

Introduction

I wanted to take him back.

It was just for a moment as I sat in dark chaos, or maybe in a bathtub full of bubbles.

I'm acutely aware I'm not supposed to write this. I wasn't even supposed to think it, but there I was, the thoughts racing through my mind. I couldn't do it. The crying, the spit-up, and the diaper changes weren't the issue. I think it was the constant requirement of my full self for an uncountable number of days ahead.

I thought about how odd it all was. I'd done extensive training to dress up in the mouse costume at Chuck E. Cheese. Entry into clubs and jobs and educational opportunities required me to prove myself in some way, and yet every day across the world, mothers and fathers are sent home with babies, and they've had to jump through no hoops. They've had to pass no tests. It is the largest responsibility with the least number of requirements that we ever encounter.

I wasn't qualified. Didn't they know? Couldn't they tell? I didn't have the grit, the knowledge, the knack, the stamina, or the mental fortitude. It doesn't matter—here's your baby.

Out of desperation, I called my friend Samantha. She had done this before. Twice. She told me, "It will be easier in six weeks." I assured her I wouldn't survive that long.

So I pondered returning him. But where? To the hospital? People return things all the time, don't they? I've seen people with opened bags of chicken wings and even used mattresses standing in the return line at Costco. There they are happily greeted by someone in a red vest who all too casually snatches their returns and asks zero questions beyond if they'd like cash back or for the refund to be put back on their credit card.

This thought of returning him was the briefest of thoughts, flying in and out of my mind like the frantic bat that once flew into our home, causing some havoc and screaming, only to quickly return to the night sky from whence it came.

The brief thought turned into a dream in which I announced to my family that I had returned our first baby. They were livid. Incredulous. But what could I do? It had nothing to do with his worthiness but solely pointed to my own flaws and shortcomings. I told them I just didn't have it in me. The well of strength I needed wasn't deep enough.

That dream helped me sort through the gaping ineptitude I felt.

Parenthood digs down deep to the bottom of the basket, roots around, and firmly grabs hold of all your failures that you'd conveniently tucked away, then yanks them out and puts them on full display. Ta-da!

But after sloughing through three years of parenthood, I happened upon a secret. An answer. Hope. Throughout the persistent and often rapid changes in child development, this secret miraculously continues to work more than a decade after our family started using it.

It's a simple answer, though not necessarily an easy one. There is a difference.

This answer covers many of the modern parenting problems we face, from exhaustion to anxiety to depression to relentless pressure to overwhelm to fear to screen usage to the deep desire we have to connect with our families. It provides so many of the things we are looking for right now. We don't have to wait until tomorrow or next week for the benefits. This single solution releases the dam, and the answers come flooding in.

Relief. Joy. Connection. Respite. Delight. Preparation for an uncertain future.

They can all be found in one place, in one word: *play.*

Play? Like a board game?

Sure. But play encompasses so much more. Scratching the surface, it includes fiddling and tinkering, romps on the carpet, fast-paced chasing games, fantasy worlds that are carefully created and enhanced over many years, and towers of blocks. Play is those times you catch a child fully immersed in a world of his own, but what he is doing is odd by every standard of adult measurement. It has become foreign to you at your age. You wouldn't do it. But the handful of dirt he spreads across his legs and then brushes off with a stick, all on a repeating loop, is play. Strange as it all may seem, it remains a worthy use of time.

I meet moms all over the country who come up to me, tears streaming down their faces, expressing gratitude for the freedom they've found in the 1000 Hours Outside movement I coined and started in 2013. I've also met anxious grandmothers who share, often in hushed tones but with a sense of immediacy, how desperately their grandchildren need this.

Where did play go? How has childhood changed so rapidly? How did it transform into an unrecognizable entity? So many things are the same: the cereal bowls, the stories, the bath-time giggles. But so many are different: the lengthened school days, the homework that has spread its tentacles into earlier grades, the immersive video game environments, the cell phone apps, the sheer number of extracurricular opportunities. How did we get here, and what parts of these cultural changes should we embrace? Our understanding of the present—and even of the future—begins in the past.

Play connects us to all those who have gone before us, to humanity itself.

Today, in this present moment, as you read these words while the water for the macaroni and cheese boils over (that wooden spoon trick has never worked for me), and while tiny fingers grab at your pants leg, and while hopeful little eyes connect with your tired ones, play is also here to help you in the present. In the right now. In the desperation.

And wouldn't you know, while you are laying a deep foundation for your children that reaches back through all of time, and while you are allowing some of that pressure and anxiety of today's mountains to lift and rise, floating off like the clouds, you are also doing the very best thing to help your kids prepare for an uncertain future. There is nothing better than what many would consider old-fashioned play to prepare today's youth for the unknowns of tomorrow.

It is predicted that by 2030, 85 percent of the jobs that will be available haven't even been created yet. An example is swarm robots. They are exactly what they sound like—a group of fully autonomous robots that move in to accomplish tasks that used to employ people. Swarm robots are not just on their way; they are here and already being used in search and rescue, supply chain management, agriculture, and military reconnaissance.[1] Someday soon, they may be headed your way to paint the exterior of your home. Children who have been bathed in ample amounts of unstructured and semi-structured play will be equipped with the inner resources needed to navigate and handle the rapid techno-logical changes that will accompany their futures.

In generations gone by, kids used to play until the street-lights came on. How many times have you heard that phrase about playing outside until it got dark?

And yet, somewhere along the line, we passed play off as frivolous. We looked around us and started biting our fingernails, nervous about what we might be missing. The neighborhood kids were taking French horn lessons and a foreign language, practicing ballet and baseball, and running for student government. It would be irresponsible to leave our dinner dishes in the sink and toss a baseball around until the fireflies emerge and the streetlights come on, wouldn't it? Aren't there so many more worthwhile uses of our time? Those spelling words and multiplication tables aren't going to memorize themselves.

But what if there was a way to have it all—a connection to the past with a full and lively present that simultaneously prepares kids for the future?

The pages ahead will offer help and hope, giving you foun-dational life principles to come back to time and time again, even as the world around us continues to change.

You *can* slow down. You *can* enjoy today. You *can* be pres-ent. And just as important, you *can* feel confident in knowing that extended periods of play are doing wonders for your child and your family. The wave of relief you've been hop-ing for is here. The answers you've been grasping for lie in the pages ahead.

So let's dive in and explore the benefits of play. Let's dis-cover how we can do less and still gain more. Let's reclaim childhood and parenthood all at the same time. It doesn't have to be as hard as we make it. We can do this together, and we can create lasting change for generations to come.

one

A Great Divide

The Widening Chasm between Virtual and Real

Welcome to the future, which begins in the past.

Jerry Kaplan

For three years I felt like an abysmal failure. Each day came and went, and throughout all the minutes and the hours I was drowning in the needs of young children. No one really knew. Drowning often happens silently, you know.

Other moms seemed to gracefully transition into their new roles like classically trained ballerinas. I joined in the fun with three left feet. I never managed to get the infant schedules to work or the meal plans mastered. I tried all the things—mommy-and-me programs, sensory bins, exersaucers, Play-Doh, cartoons, "new" toys from mom-to-mom sales, sand tables, water tables, and train tables. So many tables. I tried making snacks that looked like *The Very Hungry Caterpillar*. I made muffin-tin lunches.

It didn't matter whether I had one, two, or three kids—I couldn't keep up with the relentless onslaught of needs that accompanied the sweetest little beings I'd ever known.

I wasn't good at this. Period.

When our oldest son turned eighteen months old, I started weekly letter activities with him. In retrospect, I have no idea why I did this. What propelled me to think, *Now is the time*? He was one and a half, we also had a newborn, and yet I had Pinterest boards filled with letter-of-the-week activities. It was like some imaginary shotgun fired in my mind, signaling the start of a race. *Go! Now! Letter A!*

For some unknown reason, I decided to share our letter adventures with friends, family, and people who barely knew me via social media. In the deep recesses of my Facebook feed lies a photo of an apple tree made from green construction paper, a paper plate, and a paper towel tube. I built it. And our one-year-old added a few apple stickers to the greenery. A picture of our (my?) masterpiece can still be found in the "*A* week" photo album, which I created a mere three months after my son learned how to walk. It's a wonder I had any friends at all.

What It's Really Like

When the doctor hands you your baby, they also hand you the weight of the world. You're sent home and left to grapple with how to fill the time that looms ahead of you, how to keep your own blood pressure in check while you're surrounded by cries of discontentment, and how to live well without a wink of sleep—all while trying to slow down the hands of the clock because the minutes are rapidly ticking away.

The pressure is on to prepare your child for college. That starts early, you know. The neighbor kids can already count to three hundred, play the cello—oh, and did I mention they're bilingual? My homemade apple tree arts and crafts projects weren't going to cut it. Or at least that's how I felt. Maybe that's why I started them so early, to cover up for perceived incompetence.

In those early days, an easy answer surfaced: *Dora the Explorer*. Dora seemed to solve all the problems, giving me a chance to actually catch my breath and to fill a small portion of the minutes of our day. Besides, our kids were learning Spanish. They could say, "Vámanos!"

There was only one snag—the show was the shortest twenty-two minutes I'd ever experienced. I'd entered some sort of time warp. How on earth could over a third of an hour evaporate so quickly?

During those days, Dora was the perfect answer—until she wasn't. I learned her magic worked only during the twenty-two minutes she was on, and then the memory of her wreaked havoc on the rest of our day. There was wailing and gnashing of teeth when I turned her off. Adding one cartoon to our day caused the remainder of our day (and many more days that followed) to be filled with requests for more and for other cartoons. I found myself, in those fleeting twenty-two minutes, scrambling and stressing or zoning out and getting nothing done at all. Dora wasn't the perfect answer; she wasn't the answer at all.

All throughout those early years of motherhood, I'd stumble to the bathroom at the end of most days with time only to brush my teeth before falling into bed, emptied and depleted. I remember looking at myself in the mirror one day, thinking this was not how I'd imagined my life. The frazzled, haggard, and sometimes depressed places I found myself in were not part of the plan. I desperately wanted to enjoy my time with my kids. Instead, I was living in a state of complete overwhelm, questioning all my daily decisions.

One afternoon, on an almost-fall Michigan day, my friend Angela asked us to go on an outside excursion with her and her kids for four hours. It was a seemingly innocuous request. She was trying something new. She'd been influenced by British educator and reformer Charlotte Mason, who recommended kids be outside for four to six hours a day whenever the weather was tolerable. Angela asked if we could bring a picnic lunch and meet them at a local park from nine in the morning until one in the afternoon.

I told her we were in, but I was skeptical. To be completely honest, I was slightly terrified. Every activity I set before my children lasted half the time it took to prepare, at best, so you can imagine how I thought the outing would go. *Four hours of misery coming right up*, I thought. What were our kids possibly going to do for all that time without a train table, a sand table, action figures, Play-Doh, and a cartoon episode at the ready? How would we manage this stripped-down excursion where we just simply wentoutside?

The next morning, I packed lunches and snacks, tracked down stray shoes, and soothed toddler outbursts, and we hustled out the door. Angela picked out a spot at the park, and we each spread our picnic blankets on the sun-drenched grass. Sorely in need of some adult connection, we sat close together, holding our infants. We had one of those friendships forged by struggling through new stages of life together—mothers in the trenches. At the time, we each had babies who were completely content to be held amid the gorgeous surroundings of a simple day in nature. We caught up on life, and the babies alternated between nursing, sleeping, and observing the subtleties of nature that vied for their attention.

We each had two older kids as well, toddlers and pre-schoolers. What did the older kids do during that time, you might wonder? To my utter surprise, they played for the entirety of those 240 minutes. Without the daily onslaught of things I threw at them in my failed attempts for a little peace and quiet, they played with the materials Mother Nature had expertly crafted for them. They reached into the depths of themselves and pulled out their imaginations.

Nature play wasn't just good for my kids that day. Oh no. For the first time in three years, I was able to enjoy some mid-day adult conversation, with a melodious backdrop of birds singing and trees rustling. The sun felt warm on my skin. I inhaled deeply, feeling the weight I'd carried on my shoulders begin to dissipate.

After three grueling years, this was the first good day I'd had as a mom.

I won't ever forget the intricacies of the setting. What I would learn over the coming years is that almost every outdoor event stuck with me, memorialized in my mind whether I'd taken a slew of pictures or not. There's something about the types of experiences that engage all the senses, the ones that pull us out of our daily routine. They stick, like the sticky foot pads of tree frogs, which are partially made of snot—a good thing to know if one happens to jump onto your arm as you traipse through the woods.

There was a vast difference between how I expected this little outing to go and how it actually went in real time. I had braced for it to go completely off the rails. What I expected to be an abysmal flop turned out to be a catalyst for transformative changes in our lives. On that day, I was simply in awe.

Our kids fell asleep in the car on the drive home. I was noticeably more relaxed and refreshed. I felt happy and fulfilled.

I'd watched my kids play that day, wondering, *Why didn't we do this sooner?* Though we had spent time outside, it was always a leftover thing, thrown into our day between library visits, gymnastics classes, and shuffling kids to and from playdates. Going outside was an afterthought in our overscheduled days. That day at the park with our friends was purposely built around playing outside in nature, and it felt entirely different.

After that day, I canceled most of the programs our kids were involved in and started to meet outside with a few other families two or three times a week. We built those days around Charlotte Mason's recommendation as best we could, looking ahead at the weather for the most "tolerable" days.

What I quickly learned is that I had been searching for the answers I needed in all the wrong places. Nature and empty space set aside for playing became my saving grace—they offered a solution to the overwhelm, overstimulation, and guilt that clouded my life. To go from barely surviving to thriving in most facets of life usually takes considerable time and effort, but sustainable change happened for myself and our kids with just one simple shift: prioritizing play.

Little did I know it at the time, but these experiences would lay the foundation for the 1000 Hours Outside movement I'd start just two years later—a movement to inspire families to bring balance between nature time and screen time back to childhood (and even adulthood).

We tend to think we need more: more entertainment, more materials, more planning, more discipline around technology, more things to buy to keep our kids and ourselves happy, content, and competent. But nature is all around us, offering respite from our demanding schedules and overstimulated minds. Though the power of nature is always available to us, many of us don't know that we can deeply trust its offerings or bask in its care. We tend to discount nature play as a tried-and-true remedy for our anxious, over-scheduled lives. We have trouble believing that simple play could be pivotal in preparing our kids for a complex future and helping us enjoy happier, more connected relationships as families today.

With all the progress that's being made to improve our lives, how have we missed this truth? Why are we moving farther away from a life of slowness and careening ever more quickly to as much and as fast as possible?

A Small Glimpse of What Has Changed

There are very few of us with life circumstances that have allowed us a front-row seat to generational changes. Many of us feel the shift, like tectonic plates that spread, slip, and collide in the earth's lithosphere, but it's hard to put a finger on exactly what is going on.

When I was a child, I roamed the neighborhood with my siblings and friends in the afternoons, on the weekends, and in the summer. We were unaccompanied and untracked by GPS devices—a situation that is rather unheard of these days, as is evidenced by Mike Lanza's book *Playborhood*. Lanza advocates turning the neighborhood where you live into a place for play. You know, kind of how things used to be.

But we weren't privy to the adult conversations and conventions of wisdom at the time, so when the cultural landscape shifted, it was hard to know why. Were the shoo-out-the-door parents misinformed? Were they blissfully ignorant of what it takes to prepare a child for future adulthood? Were they negligent, blatantly ignoring the risks that lay beyond their doorsteps?

Think back to your own childhood years. What stands out? What were the moments that made you feel most alive? What are some of your favorite memories from decades past?

The ordinary, unglamourous moments of childhood—an afternoon on a rope swing, snowball fights, and feeling the prickly grass underfoot—no longer dot the landscape of childhood. They've all but vanished, even though for so many of us who grew up before screens were so dominant, these memories still conjure up feelings of peace and satisfaction decades later, pointing to a unique power in simple moments.

We're raising children in a world bursting with technology that is in large ways shaped by corporations that spend every waking moment trying to facilitate their definition of "connection." We live in a time when fear of the future pushes us to fill every bit of blank calendar space. Are daisy chains and childhood games like Red Rover obsolete, relegated to live only in our memories? Or should these simple things still hold a place in our everyday lives? Who ultimately holds the answers to those questions?

I don't know the ins and outs of all the changes, but I do know that by the time I became a parent, I was consumed with looking for enrichment opportunities in the form of courses and classes. The local Parks and Recreation department sent me brochures every season, the libraries were running programs, and when I looked around me, that's what everyone else seemed to be doing too.

There are always changes that coincide with generations. Dr. Jean Twenge, an American psychologist who specializes in generational differences, notes in her book *iGen* that certain changes carry positive consequences while others carry negative consequences, and still others are neutral in their impact.

So, what of this onslaught of pressure to transform childhood into an adult training ground? It swept in through the back door and locked the front door. You're only allowed out through the garage to get in the minivan and head off to soccer practice, then dance, then violin practice. Is this busyness, this filling of the days, one of those changes that is positive? Is it leading to more fulfillment and greater life satisfaction? Is it neutral, having no bearing on anything at all? Or are there some negative consequences that have attached, like the burrs that stick to your pants on a walk through the woods?

Psychotherapist and school counselor Thomas Kersting joined my podcast, *The 1000 Hours Outside Podcast*, on episode 13 to discuss his book *Disconnected: How to Protect Your Kids from the Harmful Effects of Device Dependency.* Kersting is one of those individuals who, due to his line of work, has been able to personally observe generational changes. In 2008, he worked with a teen who was diagnosed with attention deficit hyperactivity disorder (ADHD). Up until that point, the average age of ADHD diagnosis was eight. In his job at a public high school, Kersting had never before worked with someone who had received a diagnosis as a teen. Kersting put it this way: "After that meeting and for the rest of that school year, literally every single request was for a teenager that had been diagnosed with ADHD. That got my wheels spinning."[1]

Angela Hanscom, pediatric occupational therapist, author of *Balanced and Barefoot*, and founder of TimberNook, which focuses on nature-centered developmental programming in New England, shares her own eye-opening path of generational changes. She saw waiting lists for childhood occupational therapy services continue to grow until they were sometimes up to a year long. I've spoken with Angela on several occasions, both on my podcast and during other small online events we have done together, and she often brings up the huge caseloads that pediatric occupational therapists carry.

When Angela speaks with crowds, she frequently asks them to think about how much outdoor play they got as children and figure out an approximate number of hours. "The typical response I get is about four to five hours of outdoor play," she says.[2] My experience as a child growing up in the 1980s and 1990s included hours of outside experiences most days of the week. I had a mile walk to school and back. My elementary school had three recesses a day that lasted somewhere between forty-five minutes to an hour each. And I spent countless afternoons and evenings playing catch in our front yard or riding my bike around the block.

The amount of time kids spend outside is one of those generational shifts from which pediatric occupational therapists are seeing the downstream effects. This is not one of those neutral generational changes. Angela says, "A half an hour a week is not enough for the children to be able to regulate themselves and be able to strengthen their muscles. Kids were starting to be more and more clumsy, falling out of their chairs at school, running into each other, running into the walls, even falling off playground equipment."[3]

Still another change that Ivy League–educated psychologist Dr. Nicholas Kardaras noticed is that some of the young children he was working with had lost the ability to play with blocks. With a number of blocks placed in front of them, these children had somehow lost that internal drive to stack, to build, and to knock down. Their curiosity had been "hijacked," as Kardaras put it.[4]

American writer, psychologist, and ventriloquist Dr. Susan Linn (you may have seen her on *Mr. Rogers' Neighborhood*) has noticed a similar trend. She states, "I can no longer assume that children know how to play creatively."[5]

Beyond the capacity to play, Kardaras also mentioned some other alarming trends in his book *Glow Kids*, such as a study out of the University of Tübingen that showed how over a twenty-year period we have lost 1 percent of our sensory awareness every year. He said, "15 years ago people could distinguish 300,000 sounds; today many children can't go past 100,000. Twenty years ago the average subject could detect 250 different shades of a particular color. Today the number is 130."[6]

Beyond the dulling of the senses, Kardaras points to a study done in 2000 (years before the release of the iPhone) that "children between the ages of 10 and 17 will experience nearly one-third fewer face-to-face interactions with other people throughout their lifetimes as a result of their increasingly electronic culture, at home and in school."[7] Cal Newport, in his book *Digital Minimalism*, warns us, "We should treat with great care any new technology that threatens to disrupt the ways in which we connect and communicate with others. When you mess with something so central to the success of our species, it's easy to create problems." He continues, "Our sociality is simply too complex to be outsourced to a social network or recued to instant messages and emojis."[8]

Kardaras echoes Kersting when he cites an 800 percent increase in ADHD in the last three decades, and he uses the phrase "stimulation dependence" in describing many of today's youth.[9] We live in what has been coined an "attention economy," where companies are massively profiting off how much of our time and attention they can commandeer.

I think one reason why grandmothers flock to our 1000 Hours Outside booth when I speak at conferences is because they too have been front-row spectators of these generational changes. Of course, there are many positives to the technologies we all enjoy, and there are legitimate necessities that require the use of technology for health, safety, and more. It's not this part that concerns the grandparents. It's the imbalance that has arisen since they were parents that has them concerned—both for their grandkids, who they don't see playing, and for their own children, who have morphed into parents bubbling over with stress. The grandmas are searching for answers they can share with their grown children who now have children of their own. Often the premise of 1000 Hours Outside is just what they are looking for.

I love talking with people from older generations and hearing about their childhoods. It's interesting to compare then versus now. A host at a campground my family was staying at a few summers back had grown up in the 1940s and spoke of getting off the school bus at the end of the school year, immediately taking off his shoes, running home barefoot, and not putting another pair of shoes on again until a new school year started in the fall.

I've talked with many who grew up in a similar time as that camp host who speak of how it was the norm to shield children from adult-centered topics. It was common to turn off radio programs or stop conversations when children came in the room because whatever was being discussed was deemed inappropriate for the ears of young people. And yet, these same kids often had free range in their neighborhoods and towns. The concern for emotional safety superseded that of physical safety.

Today we find ourselves in the reverse trend. The author of *Simplicity Parenting* and a number of other influential books, Kim John Payne speaks on how "too much, too soon" has become normalized in today's childhood.[10] We don't let our kids out of our sight, but we hand them the entire world of the internet at the average age of ten and four months.[11] "Too much, too soon" as it pertained to information was not the typical experience in generations prior. Yet these same kids played for hours outdoors without supervision, and the tales they tell often leave us with gaping mouths.

Dr. Peter Gray ends his book *Free to Learn* with a story that today would seem shocking, and he also spoke about it on my podcast. He and his wife gave their son permission to travel alone from America to Europe for two weeks in the 1980s. His son, spurred on by an interest in Dungeons and Dragons, wanted to see in person some of the places he had learned about. He brought the proposal to his parents, telling them that he would work a summer job and earn all the money needed. He would also research the ticket purchase and lodging accommodations. All he needed from them was a ride to and from the airport because . . . he was only thirteen years old. With no cell phones or GPS tracking, the Gray parents had to be satisfied with just a few short collect-call conversations over the course of a two-week period before their son made his way back home.[12]

Today the parenting norms often ban tree climbing, games of tag, and walking through the neighborhood to a friend's house, yet on the flip side we are handing kids full access to the internet at younger ages. As I write this, the average age of cell phone ownership is ten. These powerful devices, which weren't originally intended to wield so much power, have entered elementary schools. The iPhone was supposed to be a marriage of a phone and the iPod digital music player. Today a phone can track every location we've ever been to, and it is a stand-in for our camera, computer, flashlight, GPS, calculator . . . and it can work as a level.

Those born after the year 2000, also known as "digital natives," can hardly even comprehend life without constant connection. Of course, we are concerned with computer literacy as well as literacy in the more traditional sense. But have these cultural forces, invisible to most of us, pushed us in a better direction, or are they upending the quality of our current and future lives?

The History of Our Screens

The inventor of the very first screen, the television, was a farm boy named Philo Taylor Farnsworth, who lived a majority of his childhood without any electricity. In 1927, at the age of twenty-one, Farnsworth figured out how to manipulate electrons, line upon line, in such rapid succession that the human eye would see all of them as one picture.

Interestingly, many technology moguls following Farnsworth tout similar childhoods—ones completely devoid of the very mechanisms they went on to invent, refine, and ultimately massively profit from. Steve Jobs, cofounder of Apple, didn't set eyes on a computer until he was twelve years old. Microsoft founder Bill Gates had a childhood filled with hands-on living as a Boy Scout. He carved things out of wood, wove baskets, and even completed a fifty-mile hike while wearing a forty-two-pound backpack. Interestingly, many of those same tech moguls and executives went on to raise their children mostly tech-free or, at the very least, severely limited tech's influence in their children's lives.

The twenty years after Farnsworth first lined up all those electrons would come and go with very few American families owning a television—just eight thousand homes had them in 1946. Poll numbers from this time period indicate most Americans didn't even know what a television was.

What happened next can be likened to an explosion. Within a decade, the number of households with televisions would grow from the thousands to the millions. In the 1960s, there were fewer than thirty hours of programming for children available each week, mainly confined to Saturday mornings. By the 1980s, the television was blaring for more than fifty hours a week in the average American household, and by 2000, 98 percent of homes all across the United States had at least one television.[13] We've been engulfed—in a span of sixty years (just over two generations), we've gone from twenty-seven hours of children's programming available each week to five hundred hours of video content uploaded to YouTube every single minute.

We are drawn to screens in part because our brains are wired for novelty. We're built to seek out the new and unexpected, but historically there were large swaths of time where screens did not provide what we sought. The cartoons were over for the day, and the path ahead was clear: we'd have to find something else to do.

Today, that draw of the glowing screens is always lurking. And it's not just network television we're dealing with—we've added on computer monitors, video game systems, virtual reality headsets, tablets, smartphones, and smartwatches. We're up against a lot.

Beyond the devices themselves are the most brilliant minds that have designed screens in ways that capture our attention and turn our time into a commodity to be sold. Test subjects are hooked up to electrodes during initial phases of a game design, and gaming companies hire neuroscientists and neurobiologists to look for the subjects' blood pressure to spike to about 180 over 120 within the first few minutes of playing. Maximum arousal is the goal, which can lead to addictive behaviors.

We've been enrolled in a competition for our own attention and that of our children—and yet it's a competition we didn't sign up for. It's also one without fair rules and is lacking a lot of transparency. How is one household supposed to win against giant technology companies?

We can clearly see the results of this unfair game. Both kids and adults have become stimulation dependent. It's no wonder we're hooked on screens—they're working the way they're meant to.

Gearing Up for an Unknown Future

In a rapidly changing world, getting our kids ready for what is to come often feels like an insurmountable task. The jobs of tomorrow won't mirror the jobs of today, and neither will the skill sets needed. Automation, algorithms, and artificial intelligence are changing the landscape of the job market. Winifred Gallagher, author of *New: Understanding Our Need for Novelty and Change*, puts it this way: "Our children will work in industries that don't even exist now, doing jobs that we don't yet have the vocabulary to describe."[14] Can kids still have a childhood that includes basking in the sun and playing on tire swings? Or will that leave them ill-prepared for job titles like cyber calamity forecaster and human machine teaming manager?

To find some of our answers, we must look backward in order to look forward. What prepared Steve Jobs and Bill Gates for their transformative technology roles? Was it the technology itself, or was it the stark opposite? The fact that they were both born in 1955, more than twenty years before the home computers entered the marketplace, gives us our answer. Steve Jobs didn't use a computer at all until age twelve, and Bill Gates was thirteen before he used one for the first time.[15] Do we prepare our kids for a future that's inextricably linked to technology while still allowing them to be kids and partake in the hands-on moments of today? Can a childhood that is filled with kittens, scooters, kite flying, and drippy summer popsicles even remotely equip children for what lies ahead?

We've got one shot at this. The question looms, encircling our minds: Are we doing this right?

To be prepared for a job market that spits out changes at increasingly faster rates, our children need to be innovative, adaptive, imaginative, opportunistic, and resilient. The path to those skills does not lie in a virtual realm where kids are passive participants in two-dimensional worlds that have been preprogrammed by adults and artificial intelligence. The qualities we want to impart to our children are cultivated through self-directed play and hands-on experiences.

What a tricky predicament. Screens are, on some level, providing for our all-consuming needs. The thought of limiting or abandoning them is sometimes too much to even consider. And yet, according to a report released by the University of Michigan about how children use their time, on average, kids play outside four to seven minutes a day but use screened devices for four to seven hours each day.[16] We clearly have lost our balance. The scales have tipped. They're no longer even upright—they are falling over.

The 1000 Hours Outside premise isn't to set aside technology completely—it's not a binary choice. Rather, it's an invitation to chase after what's real, to strive for a desperately needed balance. Instead of being restricting, as in, "You must spend this many hours outside each year," the premise is inviting. You get to! The world is waiting for you!

How Did We Get Here?

We can't know what we don't know. I think many of us who have landed in this space and time—where we can buy refrigerators with built-in screens and ask Alexa to announce to our families that it's dinnertime—wonder how we arrived here in the first place. We're keenly aware that things have changed since we were kids, but we aren't sure to what extent. More importantly, does it matter? As previously mentioned, some generational changes are just that: changes. Others hold more far-reaching implications.

What I remember from childhood is that my group of peers was involved in a few after-school activities, maybe a sport and an instrument. We were all given some homework beginning in the fourth grade or so. But there was also a lot of freedom. There was television, but it wasn't unending, especially if you didn't have cable. There were video games, but they looked like baby cartoons in comparison to the immersive video games of today.

When I was a child, one of our first family computers had a whopping four gigabytes of memory that we divvied up among our family. In comparison, the current iPhone 14 offers options up to 512 gigabytes. Back then, we were beside ourselves with glee to have almost an entire gig in our individual ownership. There were squabbles when anyone went even slightly over their allotted limit. The twelve stages we were trying to defeat on the 1989 video game *Prince of Persia* were what occasionally took us over our maximum. These were the years we used terms like "CGA" and "VGA" and "Super VGA," which would be completely foreign to digital natives.

There were even mobile phones during my childhood, but they weighed over four pounds and could only make

. . . wait for it . . . phone calls. How antiquated. We moved from using pliers for changing the television channel to being able to access an unending amount of streaming content from almost anywhere in the world with the swipe of a finger. In fact, the very first smartphone had eight gigabytes of memory, completely outshining our family's third iteration of personal computer. Eight gigs all to one person. What bliss. Who could have ever imagined?

In keeping with the rapid speed of technological change, Jerry Kaplan notes in *Humans Need Not Apply* that the memory storage in today's smartphone has over one million times as much memory as the Apple II computer from 1977, which sold for almost $1,300. Taking into account inflation, that same computer today would cost around $5,800. Kaplan compares the change to the speed of a snail versus the speed of an international space station.[17]

Every eighteen months to two years, processing speed doubles what it previously was, and this trend has been going on for fifty years with no end in sight. In his book *The Tech-Wise Family*, Andy Crouch writes, "The pace of technological change has surpassed anyone's capacity to develop enough wisdom to handle it."[18] Indeed, my family would have been hard-pressed to imagine a world where we went from gleefully sharing four gigabytes to owning 128 times more than that at a fraction of the cost.

It was the electric telegraph in the 1830s that first allowed communication to travel at a speed greater than that of the human body. Neil Postman writes, "The telegraph created an audience and a market not only for news but for the fragmented, discontinuous, and essentially irrelevant news, which to this day is the main commodity of the news industry."[19]

Information consumption has skyrocketed to a whopping 11.8 hours of information received every single day for the average American.[20] We spend 75 percent of our life receiving information.[21] When I find myself in an endless scroll for any length of time, I often walk away feeling like what I saw was, as Postman put it, "fragmented, discontinuous, and essentially irrelevant."

An increased pace can have unintended consequences. Today's kids live with unrelenting pressures. To be sure, they have most of the pressures we had when we were young, yet these are often magnified many times over, and they are experiencing new ones as well. Consider the information overload they are dealing with day in and day out.

In his book *The Coddling of the American Mind*, Greg Lukianoff places a list of first-grade readiness requirements from 1979 next to a list of requirements from 2019. In 1979, St. Theresa's Catholic School in Austin, Texas, only had twelve items that were meant to decide whether a child was ready for the first grade. These included physical markers such as having two to five permanent teeth, being able to stand on one foot with eyes closed for at least five seconds, and being able to travel alone in the neighborhood (four to eight blocks) to a store, a school, a playground, or a friend's house. Here, once again, we see the theme of physical safety being much less of a concern. The academic requirements were also minimal. Three out of the twelve dealt with academics, if you can even put this first one in that category:

1. Can he draw and color and stay within the lines of the design being colored?
2. Can he count eight to ten pennies?
3. Does your child try to write or copy letters or numbers?

In 2019, the first-grade readiness requirements for a school in Austin, Texas, included thirty items. In this list the majority of the checklist revolves around academics. Some examples include:

1. Identify and write numbers to 100.
2. Count by tens to 100, by twos to 20, by fives to 100.
3. Interpret and fill in data on a graph.
4. Read all kindergarten-level sight words.[22]

Learning hasn't always been equated with books. In his book *The Disappearance of Childhood*, written in 1982, Neil Postman says, "In a world without books and schools, youthful exuberance was given the widest possible field in which to express itself. But in a world of book learning such exuberance needed to be sharply modified."[23]

We've cut off much of that youthful exuberance as we've constructed childhoods that are overscheduled and overstimulating. Parents are pressured to build their children a résumé for life, but this approach isn't adequately preparing kids for what's ahead—and it's distracting from the experience-rich childhood that kids need today.

Living in the Present Prepares Kids for the Future

We never finished my Pinterest board activities—and yet all of our kids still miraculously learned their letters. It just so happens you don't have to make a jellyfish (or a jaguar or jungle) out of the letter *j* or perform a stellar rendition of "Jack and the Beanstalk" in order to prepare for life. Thank goodness.

Childhood isn't solely about preparation for the future. It's about the present. It's about the relationships we're building day in and day out while we're packing lunches and playing board games. I want to live in the present as much as possible. I want to connect on a palpable level with our children where they are—here, right now, in our home. I want to meet their gazes, listen to their musings, and love them as they are. And herein lies the glorious thing: I believe that in doing so, in hearkening to the simple songs of our souls, we're preparing them for the unknown.

Relationships are central to a rich life. Tom Hobson writes in *Teacher Tom's Second Book*, "Getting along with our fellow humans is the real secret to future employment, not to mention happiness."[24] Kim John Payne writes something similar in *Simplicity Parenting*: "The primary predictor of success and happiness in life is our ability to get along with others."[25]

A life filled with loving relationships will be broad and rich, and yet, though we're more connected than ever before through technology, many of us still lack meaningful attachment. Ironically, Mark Zuckerberg, who cofounded the social media platform Facebook, is on a path to implementing a metaverse, a virtual place where we will "lose ourselves" and "not want to leave," and that will be "the primary way we spend our time." He's creating this virtual world that we ostensibly won't want to leave because he wants to "enable people to engage with one another."[26] Hmm. That doesn't seem to make sense. Maybe we don't need this "help," as humanity has been seeking connection since time immemorial.

Johann Hari brings up a good point in his book *Stolen Focus*. If social media companies really desire to bring us together, why don't they show us through their apps where our friends are physically? Then we could go see them and say "Hi!" face-to-face. Bring the card games and some queso. Let's go for a walk. But then we would have to put our phones down and close the apps that are meant to capture our eyeballs and equate to a bottom-line profit model that requires us to stay put.

When reality is no longer the primary "real" in our lives, we reach a scary crossroads. Is being overtaken by technology inevitable? Should we throw in the towel? Or should we fight those feelings of inevitability with a push for staying in the present as much as possible?

Only 35 percent of teenagers socialize face-to-face anymore. The remainder of them communicate via screens.[27] During a conversation, eye contact is needed 60 to 70 percent of the time in order to build an emotional connection (though this may vary due to cultural norms). Yet the average adult today only makes eye contact between 30 to 60 percent of the time in a typical conversation.[28] Are handheld devices at play here? How well are screens truly enabling us to engage with each other on a meaningful level? By many measures, the effect seems to be one of social illusion rather than deep connection.

Technology creeps in, and then it takes over. We've seen it time and time again. And it's creeping in faster and faster. Older technologies took decades to sweep through culture. Eighty years passed before the telephone was a part of thirty-five million American households. The automobile slid into that many homes in fifty years. The radio needed only twenty-five years, the television just ten. Apple's iPhone, which launched midyear in 2007, sold almost seventy-two million phones by 2011. It more than doubled what the telephone did in eighty years . . . in less than five. Integration is happening at a breakneck speed.

But nature holds the same capacity to creep in and take over. It's relentless too. It doesn't give up. It knows its rightful place. Even in a parking lot washed over with concrete, nature will relentlessly push through the narrow cracks and crevices. And from nature, we can draw some resolve as parents. In order to prepare our children for the future and enjoy our lives with them today, the key is to step back to a slower pace, leaving margin for play and exploration so that we can go forward.

Imagine swinging in a hammock with your child, sprawling out on a picnic blanket with some of your favorite books and games, making a flip-book, creating worlds out of blocks, or hiking to a waterfall with its thunderous sounds and having the assurance that this is enough. You can preserve and protect your relationship with your child. You can fully enjoy their company while at the same time prepare them for the future.

While they may not overtly state it, big-technology businesses essentially view us as products. They profit off our time and attention in the form of advertising dollars. When we return to play, we step out of a business model that is meant to keep us stuck and sedentary. When our lives are filled with all the things that make us feel fully human, we begin to run out of time for screens and shake free from the grasp of the tech overlords.

The chasm is widening. Virtual experiences are making a good run at seeming real, but we know deep down that they are not the same. Even immersive technologies that surround us with content don't satisfy in the same way as a cup of tea with a friend or a gulp of fresh air in the winter does. The ever-increasing chasm may make us feel like we have to choose one side or the other or we will free-fall in the middle. That is not the case. We can plant ourselves firmly where we want to be and build an ever-expanding bridge to the other side, visiting only when we want or need to. An awareness of the past gives us a better understanding of what we need to be vigilant about today, and it gives us hope that no matter what rapid changes are yet to come, humanity still reigns supreme.

Discussion Questions

1. Share a few of your favorite memories from childhood.
2. Talk about some childhood memories where adults weren't present or directing your play. How did you feel about those times? Do you look back on those memories fondly?
3. In what ways is the childhood of your child (or grandchild) different from yours? Which of these differences strikes you as positive? Which strikes you as negative?

Action and Adventure Prompts

1. Talk to someone from a previous generation and learn about their childhood. Make a book that displays some of the main differences between their generation and yours.
2. If it fits with your culture, set a timer and have a conversation where you try to maintain eye contact 60 to 70 percent of the time. Talk about how this feels.
3. Print out a free 1000 Hours Outside tracker at 1000HoursOutside.com/Trackers and start being intentional about filling your year with real-life experiences.

two

Slow Down and Gain More

What Happens When You Stop Believing Play Is Frivolous

We have created a false dream and called it Progress.

John Holt, *Escape from Childhood*

I'd like to introduce you to Watson. He's not a person; he's a supercomputer. And the label "super" is rather an understatement. Designed by IBM, Watson has raced past mastering the game of chess with its mere finite combinations of moves (though this finite number is more than the number of atoms in our observable universe) and has moved on to a more challenging game, *Jeopardy!* This popular trivia game show has more open-ended dilemmas than where to move your pawn, like how much to wager for a daily double. No worries, though. Watson the supercomputer has consumed over *two hundred million* pages of text. That's equivalent to about a million books. (How many of those could you fit in your built-ins?) Not surprisingly, Watson crushed the *Jeopardy!* competition because it can sift through and analyze those two hundred million pages in under three seconds.[1]

I love to read. I love the weight of a book in my hand. I have a favorite size of book, I have a favorite paper color (cream, please), and my surroundings are always filled with stacks of the ideas and experiences of others wrapped up in a book. My purse is filled with books. I never travel without one (usually I have three), even if I know I'll hardly be able to fit in any paragraphs, let alone chapters. If there's even an off chance that I'll be able to read, I make sure I have books with me.

If I have seventy good years of being able to read one book every single day, that amounts to only about twenty-five thousand books. I should mention that it's a struggle to read one book every single week.

We are desperately behind the pace set by technology, with no chance to ever catch up. Though we may not know of Watson in particular or of other comparable technological advances, we can still sense the widening divide. Dear Watson can fly through the information of forty two-hundred-page books read every single day for a life span of seventy years, all in under three seconds—or, for comparison, in about the time it takes to sneeze. *Ah-choo.* You just lost at *Jeopardy!*

How will our children ever be able to compete when humans and machines aren't even in the same arena anymore? The obvious answer is to hustle, isn't it? Stuff more in. Read more, study more, practice more. Faster, please.

Everything Moves So Fast

There is something about the speed of everyday life, which swirls around us in a frenetic, sometimes hard-to-catch-your-breath pace, that seems to be changing how we parent.

It was less than two centuries ago that information could travel only at the speed of people. Some people were able to deliver information on horseback and eventually others via steam locomotives, but all transfer of information for most of human history had a limit of about thirty-five miles per hour. Today, researchers out of the University of Southampton have created optic fibers that move data almost at the speed of light. They're 99.7 percent of the way to moving it that fast![2] The thoroughbreds and choo-choo trains have been surpassed in a way that is utterly incomprehensible.

We may not be working in the fields that are creating these cutting-edge technologies, but so many of us are benefactors of them daily. You can order taco shell toasters on Amazon, and they'll come tomorrow! They might even come later this afternoon. Either way, they will be placed directly on your doorstep, ready to take your tacos to the next level.

We used to have to drive to Bed, Bath & Beyond with our 20 percent coupons, walk the aisles, track down an elusive sales associate to find the taco shell toasters amid the floor-to-ceiling shelves of products, walk back up to the front of the store, twiddle our fingers in line while one customer attempted a return and another paid with a check, and then transport our purchase home. All without 1,600 customer reviews to guide our path.

Interestingly, the name "Relentless" was a contender instead of "Amazon." In fact, if you go to the website www.Relent less.com, it takes you right to Amazon. Since the Amazon is the largest river in the world, both names seem fitting.

Even something as ubiquitous as calling kids in for dinner has taken a twist. We used to have to yell for them, and depending on the size or layout of our home, we might have to walk a few steps to where the sound of our voice would reach them. Today, Alexa can do it. She can do it quicker and easier because she can broadcast to everyone all at once.

This is not to downplay the importance and allure of speed when it comes to technology. Our family uses Google Maps on a regular basis to help us take adventures. This isn't simply a case of avoiding a return to MapQuest and printing out directions, or even going a little farther back to pulling out an impossible-to-refold paper map. This newer technology helps us find locations, both outdoor and indoor, that are a good fit for our family. By searching for things like "waterfall," "nature center," "nature preserve," "trailhead," "beach," "state park," and "playground," we can find what's out there to explore! We can also look ahead of time at both reviews and pictures to make informed choices about the places we might visit. The antiquated way was looking through AAA travel books that had no reviews and no pictures, a case of less information and yet more time invested.

When we live in this whirlpool of information, it is helpful in so many facets of life. Yet accompanying this torrent of high speeds is a prodding to speed up everything else in our lives.

Erin Loechner, a blogger, a speaker, and the founder of the international homeschooling co-op Other Goose, wrote an insightful book called *Chasing Slow*. The title alone reminds us that slow doesn't come easy. It isn't the default setting. We must chase after it again and again. In our culture, we must relentlessly pursue downtime. It is harder to slow down than it is to speed up.

In a world where Watson can process information quicker than we can even comprehend, there is an underlying pressure that we must move quickly too. There are transformational experiences waiting for our children in the after-school photography club (or cooking club, chess club, foreign language club, STEM club, creative writing club, watercolor painting club, video game club, or investment portfolio club). Hurry! Don't delay! Sign up for it all. We feel like we need to dump more information into our kids' brains because technology is taking the lead.

In a fashion similar to after-school programs, schools have continued to extend their tentacles into the corridors of our homes, and it seems as though we should welcome them right in. We're just trying to keep up, aren't we? Being in school close to six hours per day, 180 days per year, for twelve or thirteen years just isn't enough—you must complete homework as well. The National Center for Education Statistics found that high schoolers get an average of 6.8 hours of homework per week, and elementary students get just shy of five hours.[3]

This has the trappings of a race. Someone blew the whistle. You may have even heard it at your first ultrasound. And once you're off, legs and arms pumping, hair blowing in the breeze, carrying your children under your arms, there's no looking back—or even around you. This race is individual, and you better get your kids to the finish line as quickly as possible, leaping hurdles as you go.

Simon Sinek reminds us in his book *Infinite Game* that life is actually not like these individual races we feel we were thrown into. There are no winners in marriage, in child-rearing, in business. Who, in the course of all humanity, has "won" marriage? Who has won the gold medal in parenting?[4]

We have lists like *Forbes*'s "30 under 30" and *Fortune*'s "40 under 40," where we can learn about the "hottest rising stars in business," which also reinforce this notion of more and faster. Time is running out. You're getting old, and quickly. But is there really a career winner? One to rule them all? Surely, there are standouts—Thomas Edison, Henry Ford, Steve Jobs, Elon Musk. But I've never seen a race that has more than one winner, so this view of life, this view of childhood, is inaccurate at best and quite damaging at worst. The purpose of life is not to win. It's to keep going.

Early childhood professional Magda Gerber puts it this way: "Childhood is not a race to see how quickly a child can read, write, and count. It is a small window of time to learn and develop at the pace that is right for each individual child. Earlier is not better."[5]

Earlier is not better.

But isn't it? Our society is enamored with the child prodigy. When we learn that Mozart was performing internationally on the harpsichord at age five, but our kid still wets the bed occasionally at age eight, it's all too easy to feel like we are losing at something.

Interestingly, Mozart's accomplishments fly in the face of the ten-thousand-hours-to-mastery concept put out by Malcolm Gladwell in his book *Outliers*. The rule is that it takes around ten thousand hours of intensive practice to achieve mastery of complex skills, and yet it is unlikely Mozart spent more than thirteen hours a day during his third and fourth years of life intensely practicing the harpsichord. His parents didn't take him to the most expensive lessons. He learned from his dad. And he didn't after-school-program his way into being a child prodigy. He simply was one.

This societal fascination with early achievement is another reason we feel we must explode out of the starting gate and never stop running. Yet it is estimated that only one in five million children is a prodigy. The odds aren't good, and no pushing or prodding is going to change that.

So can we race differently? Can we perhaps go the other direction? Find another finish line? Skip instead of run? Saunter instead of sprint? Kids need some of their own time in order to flourish in their growing-up years. Can we scoot around the hurdles or even knock them over instead of aiming to leap above them? Is it an act of defiance to simply step off the track completely and find a new path?

I'll never forget the first morning I woke up after high school graduation. For thirteen years, my life had looked almost identical to that of my peers. Sure, there were some minor variances. Some played sports while others didn't. Some rode the bus while others drove their own cars. But for the most part we all marched to the same rhythm for almost the entirety of childhood. Yet once we were handed that diploma, life diverged. In a matter of a few months, we went from being all together to being dispersed like milkweed in the wind. Some went to community college, others to a university, others to trade school, others to the military, others to missions work, and others directly into the workforce. Some took a gap year. Some got married quickly, some waited years, and others never got married. Some moved out right away while others stayed around home for a little longer.

We all took one path in order to reach multiple destinations. But could we also have gotten to our individual destinations by taking our own unique paths?

The Offerings of a Slow Life

While information swirls around us just slightly slower than the speed of light, what can a slower life possibly offer us?

What does a slow life even mean? And the most pressing question of all: How can a slow life be beneficial?

There are a number of ways we will never match a machine. We won't ever measure up to Watson. So, armed with the archives of human history, a GPS map to anywhere, and a fully functional calculator in our pockets, let's take time to focus on our distinctions as human beings. One of those is having a childhood. Watson didn't get a childhood, but all of us did. And our kids get one too. But why? What is the purpose of it? Playwright Tom Stoppard says it's to be a child. So eloquently he writes, "Because children grow up, we think the child's purpose is to grow up. But a child's purpose is to be a child. Nature doesn't disdain what lives for only one day. It pours the whole of itself into each moment. We don't value the lily less for not being made of flint and built to last."[6]

Childhood is about today. It's about that small amount of growth that today provides, making way for the next day. It's not about growth for outcome's sake. It is about growth for growth's sake, for the intrinsic and thrilling value of learning just a little more and flourishing in this present time. Hopefully we've all had periods in our lives where we've gotten to grow authentically, in our own way, with no timetables or bubble Scantron test forms to fill out.

I've learned the most I've ever learned since becoming a mom. The biggest lesson has been how to let go of control, but I've learned some other practical skills along the way too. I've learned how to grow flowers, the most beautiful ones I've ever seen: Benary's giant zinnias, Grandpa Ott's morning glories, pinwheel marigolds, ladybird nasturtium, teddy bear sunflowers, copper red strawflowers. I've learned when to start the seeds in our growing zone 6A, how to thin seedlings, when to transplant, how to harvest, and how to save seeds for next year. Most flowers lose a bit of their vibrance as they dry, but did you know that the colors of dried strawflowers hardly fade over time? They are referred to as "everlastings."

It took me several years to learn the ins and outs of growing something from seed, but I was able to learn in a way that never felt rushed. It never felt comparative or anxiety filled. Instead, it was thrilling. The colors. The smells. The textures. The look of delight on my friends' faces when I showed up with a fresh bouquet of summer blooms. That was better than any A-plus I could ever have earned.

There is something to be said about intrinsic motivation— that is, learning not for the stars or the accolades but for the sheer joy of newfound knowledge. The things we learn as adults remind us there is time to learn new things, and when we are learning for the fun of it, a timeline isn't attached for mastery. Just like us, kids desire to pull away from the abstract and do something real.

So where does this rush to cram childhood with gobs of knowledge come from? Why do we commandeer so much of our children's time?

We are certainly well-intentioned. We all want what's best for our kids. The way we do modern childhood assuredly isn't easy on adults. All those extracurriculars aren't cheap, and all the carting around is eating up time.

If this onslaught of busyness isn't taking us where we thought it would, let's realize that now. A rushed and harried life, complete with a side of adult anxiety, probably isn't our ideal, and it isn't sending the greatest message to our kids.

Lillian Dickson, independent missionary, author, and speaker, said, "Life is like a coin. You can spend it any way you wish, but you only get to spend it once."[7] Do we really know what we're spending it on?

But What about College?

There is one—and only one—main thing that everyone seems to be careening toward: the prestigious college. That's it. What else would we need to race so vigorously toward?

Community college doesn't evoke the same sense of panic. Nor does trade school or a gap year. I've never heard anyone ask if such-and-such child was on track with the perfect courses and credits needed for cosmetology school. It's that Ivy League beacon of light that seems to be beckoning all of us, and it's just gotten so much harder to get in.

Or has it?

All this time and money and intense effort should do the trick.

Or will they?

That shiny Ivy League status has some tricks up its sleeve, which Linda Flanagan chronicles in her book *Take Back the Game*. In 1990, over half of those who applied at Johns Hopkins University were accepted—53 percent, to be exact. Yet just over thirty years later in 2021, the acceptance rate had dropped to 11 percent. Well, that's a big difference. Applicants went from having a fifty-fifty chance of acceptance to having only a one in ten chance. Cue the panic.[8]

Knowing nothing else about this, which I certainly didn't before reading Flanagan's book, I would've concluded that the competition has gone up dramatically. The parents who have pulled ahead are the ones who bought baby bump headphones and played music to their little ones in utero, raised them in a bilingual environment, and enrolled them in enrichment activities from dawn until dusk throughout their childhood. These parents rounded the last curve of the racetrack and, with a sudden burst of energy, left everyone else in the dust on the final sprint. So much for the rest of us who were doling out tater tots and falling asleep on the couch while we played Disney movies for our kids on repeat. Well, there's nothing we can do about it now. Our lack of creating the perfect learning conditions has doomed our children to be the nine out of ten who will receive a piece of paper in the mail with "REJECTED" stamped in red across the front.

Yet Flanagan opens our eyes to a different story. In 1983, *U.S. News & World Report* had a new idea. They decided they would rank American universities, and their list became the most highly read ranking system in all of history. Decades after their first release, which places Stanford University, Harvard University, Yale University, and Princeton University as the top four (seems like we could've guessed that), the University of Michigan conducted a study regarding how these rankings were affecting the universities. This 2010 study showed that the *U.S. News & World Report* ranking system significantly affected the universities' applications and admissions.

Another study done in 2011 by Leadership and Management showed an almost one-to-one correspondence between rankings and number of freshman applicants. When a university ranked one place higher on the list, they would see an almost one percent increase in the number of applicants.[9] That may seem like a small amount, but when universities have tens of thousands of freshman applicants, one percent represents a lot more students applying. Reaching a particular level on the college rankings board understandably became a big goal for universities.

How are these rankings determined? One of the six main factors that can bump a university up the list is selectivity. How do they increase selectivity? One way is to admit fewer students. But another clever way is to increase the number of students who apply. More applicants to fill the limited number of slots increases the selectivity.

How does a university get more students to apply? Marketing, plain and simple. This is the answer to the commonly asked question "Why am I getting so much college mail?" They want you to apply! According to Flanagan, "The average student's name is sold about 18 times over the course of his or her four years of high school."[10]

So are the neighborhood kids actually flying by our own kids, or are the universities just sending out more marketing materials than ever before, thus driving up applications in order to drive up selectivity percentages for the sole purpose of college rankings?[11] The circular game continues as the university bumps up the rankings list, the applications increase, and in turn so does the selectivity year after year. The funnel isn't narrowing as it might've originally seemed. It's all an illusion.

Ivy Coach is a company founded by college counseling expert Bev Taylor. Beginning in the tenth or eleventh grade, students are able to seek out a private college counselor like Taylor. There are thousands to choose from. Ivy Coach in particular offers many packages, but the unlimited package (which is often not chosen "typically because of the fee" that they "make no apologies for") gives these high school students the "most exclusive college counseling concierge service."[12]

Right off the bat, Ivy Coach echoes Flanagan in saying, "Receiving a brochure from a college does not in any way indicate that the college is interested in admitting you. Receiving a brochure from a college only means that the school wants you to apply. Why? Because the more students who apply, the lower the schools' admission rate will be, and the higher the school will be ranked in *U.S. News & World*

Report. That's right. Colleges—even our nation's most elite colleges—want anyone and everyone to apply. Mailing out brochures is their little way of expressing this desire."[13]

This topic of selectivity also arises in youth sports. Sports provide one of the only avenues through the murky college application process, especially if you're not able to (or didn't even know to) hire a coach to help in your conquest of the college admission process. College athletes are often recruited and admitted early, giving anxious students and parents a sigh of relief. But these early admitted athletes reduce the number of spaces left for regular admission. Ta-da! The selectivity goes up once again.

An awareness of the arena we've been thrust into hopefully allows us to pause. This knowledge helps break the spell that society seems to be under. Is this circular game one we really want to pursue beginning in early childhood? Why not wait a little instead? Or wait a lot and see where the path unfolds for our children instead of guiding them along a well-worn path others have trodden before us? Their path may include Ivy League schools, or it may not. Linda McGurk, author of *There's No Such Thing as Bad Weather*, writes, "There are plenty of ways to get ahead in life without an Ivy League education."[14] Interestingly, studies indicate that while an Ivy League education has been shown to give advantages in salary, it does "not have a notable positive impact on student learning, job satisfaction, or well being."[15]

Maybe chasing after what it appears we should be chasing after isn't the way to go. Instead, we seek the unmeasurable: youthful exuberance, long attention spans, a quest for further learning, depth of relationship—the types of things that come only through suspended time. Kim John Payne says, "Loving something for its own sake—not for its potential in fame, glory, or music scholarships—is far from ordinary. It's an exceptional blessing—a strength of character any parent would wish for their child."[16]

A slower life—one that allows us to step off the societal conveyor belt that comes to an abrupt halt once kids reach college and doesn't give much direction beyond those years— offers a broader selection of things than GPA and test results. Besides, that slower pace has the potential of affecting GPA and test results.

Cognitive processes are grounded in movement and creative play. Here's one sentence worth remembering from Dr. Carla Hannaford in her book *The Dominance Factor*: "Whenever we are moving muscles, we are stimulating and building up nerve pathways too—pathways that help us perform all sorts of tasks."[17]

Your Own Path

A slower pace, time to play outside, and having portions of the calendar set aside for board games and for read-alouds are all things that contribute to creativity, flexibility, and enjoyment in life. If we can free ourselves from the "one path to success" paradigm, our worlds can open up. If we can be confident in knowing that entrance into a prestigious college doesn't have to be the final goal for every child, we can release some of this pressure to push harder. Put the Ivy League college, the basketball trophies, and the honor roll stickers out of your sight for the time being. If you find the only reason you're doing something is for college résumé building, consider taking a hard pass. Remember how much of life there is waiting to be enjoyed and that enjoyment could be considered success.

One way our family slowed down and followed our own unique path is that our kids skipped preschool. I used to keep this a secret. Well, technically we participated in a small preschool co-op with some of my friends. We called it "Little Ones Preschool Co-op," and it was a struggle, as are many things when you're trying to coerce small children to learn in ways that are against their nature of being. All the families quit after one semester.

Our kids also skipped kindergarten. That was an even bigger secret.

In some sense I feel I was born in the wrong decade. In the 1960s, 40 percent of kids didn't go to kindergarten, so not going would have been considered fairly normal, something you didn't have to hide from everyone else. I'm just trying to revive the trend.

When we skipped preschool, I knew of only one other family who did the same. Preschool was just what you did, the next step in a series of childhood enrollment opportunities. We are not anti-preschool; the cost-benefit ratio just didn't work for our family at the time. The costs were money and hassle, while the benefits didn't seem like anything beyond what our kids were getting by playing at home and out in the community with friends. So we passed.

Then we passed on kindergarten too. We skipped over all of it, which I realize may not be the right fit for every family for a myriad of reasons. But my point as mentioned before is only this: there seem to be other paths to success.

Our youngest (fifth) child is the most recent kindergarten skipper in our family. As I write this, a new school year is right around the corner, and she is in full-on anticipation mode. Everything is new and exciting when you're a child. We're a homeschooling family, and we have a few curriculum books for her first-grade year (mind you, they are kindergarten books since we skipped that year). Her enthusiasm was so great that I pulled her math book out early. As I studied and researched to write this very book, she sat beside me, six sharpened pencils in hand, and went at her math book with gusto. In fact, over the course of a single afternoon as she came and went, returning to the math book when she desired, she finished thirteen out of the thirty weeks of lessons. She finished almost half of the entire kindergarten math book in one afternoon. Any twinge of doubt I was feeling that she might be "behind" dissipated.

Author and educator John Holt wrote a book called *Learning All the Time* with the subtitle *How Small Children Begin to Read, Write, Count, and Investigate the World, without Being Taught*, and I've seen this concept play out time and time again with our children. They've had no preschool, no kindergarten, and no formal lessons at all, and yet somehow they have learned through living how to write their numbers, how to add and subtract, how to write their names, and so much more. It's like witnessing a miracle.

According to author and teacher John Taylor Gatto, "Reading, writing, and arithmetic only take about one hundred hours to transmit as long as the audience is eager and willing to learn. The trick is to wait until someone asks and then move fast while the mood is on. Millions of people teach themselves these things—it really isn't very hard."[18] We use the "they'll do it when they're ready" approach so often with babies and toddlers: They'll roll over when they're ready. They'll crawl when they're ready. They'll take their first steps when they're ready. Is it possible to extend this approach into the early childhood years—and even beyond? Giving our kids the chance to bloom on their own timelines allows us to alleviate a lot of stress from our lives, from their lives, and from our collective family experience.

In her book *The Dominance Factor*, Dr. Carla Hannaford chronicles one way that stress affects learning. We each have a dominant side of the brain—we're often referred to as being left-brained or right-brained. Those who take a more logical and calculated approach to life are usually (but not always) left-brained, while those who tend to be more creative and spontaneous are usually right-brained. Beyond the brain, we also have a dominant hand, foot, eye, and ear. The dominant hand becomes fairly apparent by school age, but many of us have never considered our personal dominances for the other three categories.

When trying to figure out foot and ear dominance, Hannaford says to think about which foot you would lead with when walking up a set of stairs, and which ear you would turn toward a sound from across the room.[19]

Determining eye dominance is fun! The way you figure it out is by holding your thumb up directly in front of you and lining it up with a vertical object. It could be a doorframe or a window frame (in my case it's a stick of deodorant on the dresser in front of our bed). With your thumb out, you'll see two images, but when you close either eye, your thumb will magically move! Whichever open eye shows your thumb lined up with the vertical object is your dominant eye. Did you try it? Did you have your children try it?

Here are my stats. I am left-brained, right-handed, right-ear dominant, right-foot dominant, and left-eye dominant. The number of possible variations gives thirty-two different dominance profiles that are explained in detail in Hannaford's book. These profiles are interesting to know about because they affect things like the optimal place for a child to sit in a classroom.

For our discussion here, I want to focus on the concept of stress. A childhood that has transformed into an arms race for college is filled with stressors. And when we experience stress, the dominant side of our brains takes over while the nondominant part doesn't work as optimally. Our brains have a crossover pattern, meaning the left side of the brain controls the right side of the body, and vice versa. Therefore, problems can arise when a hand, eye, foot, or ear dominance lies on the same side as the dominant brain hemisphere.

In my profile, my eye dominance (left) lines up with my brain dominance. This helps explain why I have an extremely hard time reading when I'm stressed out. My left eye is the conductor for the tracking of both my eyes, and because of the brain crossover pattern, it's the right side of my brain that controls my left eye. When stress arises, the left (dominant) side of my brain takes over and the right shuts down. Out the window flies my reading comprehension.

Hannaford writes, "Under stress, the eyes tend to move outward, relying on a broad, peripheral focus in order to see where the danger is. This makes convergent eye teaming difficult, and therefore reading. Because your primary function is survival, if asked to read when stressed, the dominant eye will be looking for danger and you will read with your nondominant eye. This causes comprehension issues."[20]

Think about yourself, your kids, or other people you know. Is this ringing any bells? We have one child who shuts down verbally during stressful situations. It's not that she can't speak; it's almost as though she can't hear us. She can't seem to process what we're saying to her.

A story to illustrate this happened early one winter morning. We live on a small hobby farm near the Ann Arbor, Michigan, area and have a few beloved barn cats that we call our own. One day we were leaving before the sun came up to head south (because that's what you do when you live in Michigan and it's the middle of winter), and one of the cats must've scooted into the house as we were carrying our pillows and blankets out, trudging bleary-eyed through the darkness and swirling snow to get into our van. When we returned home from our balmy trip, we were surprised to find the cat in our house. Ever resourceful, it had gotten into the bag of cat food and found a sensory bin filled with dried, dyed chickpeas that we used for playtime. The cat had used the bin as a litter box while we were gone.

Ever since that trip, we've been more careful when leaving our house during the early morning hours. On a recent trip, our daughter remarked that she might have seen a cat in the kitchen as we were getting ready to head out the door. Everyone started peppering her with questions, and I could see that it stressed her out. Then she shut down. Her face had a rather blank stare, and it was as though she couldn't comprehend any of the words coming at her. Well, wouldn't you know, she is right-brain dominant and right-ear dominant.

Whenever your dominances line up on the same side and stress comes along, that eye, ear, foot, or hand is not going to function optimally. In a stressed state, a child may find themselves clumsier or less able to read or hear (or a combination of several things). This has considerable impact on school performance, job performance, sports, and more.

During the childhood period of high growth, optimal development is going to happen when kids are in an unstressed state. Yet a majority of children's waking hours in kindergarten through twelfth grade are spent in learning environments that include peer pressure, standardized testing, and fluorescent lights, which can cause arousal in the nervous system.[21]

The answer once again is slowing down. Kim John Payne, author of *Simplicity Parenting*, tells us that during play and downtime, kids are able to release the neurotoxins from their bodies. This is such a crucial part of childhood and life that Payne often prescribes three periods of boredom per day.

We all need a chance to release accumulated stress. It doesn't happen by accident. We have to be purposeful about providing time that isn't filled.

Payne also likens childhood to a cup sitting under a faucet. We're living in a society that advocates for turning both faucets up all the way. We are falling behind the machines, after all. This means pouring in schoolwork, extracurriculars, and other expectations and stressors that cause the cup to fill to the brim and often overflow. Payne says we have a choice. We can either turn down the faucet or spend the entirety of childhood mopping up spillage.[22]

Downtime—slowing down—also gives us time for reflection. It gives us some time to be with our own thoughts, to learn how to enjoy our own company without the dings and beeps of impeding technology.

This all seems rather counterintuitive on the surface, but peeling back some of the layers allows us to understand how, through pumping the brakes, we are able to gain what we are looking for—for our children, ourselves, and our families.

Change Changed

The Greatest Generation, or the GI Generation, includes those born between 1901 and 1924, a twenty-three-year time span. The Silent Generation, also known as the Lucky Few, is those born between 1925 and 1945. The Baby Boomers are those born between 1946 and 1964, and since then the generational time brackets have dropped to fifteen years. Gen X includes those born from 1965 to 1980, Gen Y is those born between 1981 and 1996, and Gen Z (also coined iGen for "Internet Generation" by Jean Twenge) includes birth years between 1997 and 2012. Generation Alpha is said to include those born after 2012 to around 2025. These generations are shifting faster, as is the nature of information and the speed at which we change careers.

Gone are the days when the skills needed for the job market changed on a generational time scale, when the majority of people secured a job right out of college and stayed with that company, often moving up the corporate ladder, for the entirety of their working years. Today, the average worker will change jobs twelve times in their life. That's twelve (at least) interviews, twelve adjustments to a new business culture, twelve new sets of coworkers, twelve different bosses, and twelve times to learn new skills and new directives.

There are many types of jobs that have a shelf life—an expiration date. Salespeople stopped selling the *Encyclopedia Britannica* door-to-door in 1996, and the encyclopedias themselves went out of print in 2010. NASA used to hire human computers—actual people who would use pencils and graph paper to determine things like how many rockets would be needed to launch a plane. Scissors grinders were experts at sharpening scissors or knives, and just like the encyclopedia salespeople, they would go door-to-door offering their services until their job became extinct around 1970.

Jobs and the skills needed to perform them have always been in flux. The difference is that the changes used to occur much slower than they do today. There used to be more time built in to have a better glimpse of what's coming and then adjust.

The nature of the job market is rapidly shifting, in part due to the rise in artificial intelligence. Jerry Kaplan writes in *Humans Need Not Apply*, "Imagine how smart you would be if you could see through thousands of eyes, hear distant sounds, and read every word as it is published. Then slow the world down to a pace where you can sample and ponder all of this at your leisure, and you'll get an idea of how these [artificial intelligence] systems experience their environment."[23] He goes on to say, "The nature of jobs available will shift so rapidly that you may find your skills obsolete just when you thought you were starting to get ahead."[24]

If the education conveyor belt stops at the college entrance gate, how are we supposed to manage this rapid change once we've graduated? When the very nature of change has changed, what are we to do when there are no longer prescribed steps ahead? Once again, the answer is found in downtime, in boredom, and in free play, all of which provide a flexible, creative, and adaptable mind.

When the society around us is constantly pushing for bigger and faster and stronger, what are some strategies we can use to pull back? We can begin by girding ourselves with knowledge and coming back to it often. When the pressure is coming from all sides, we need continued strength to push back against it. We need the following messages on repeat:

There are many paths to life success. There is no rush.

The increase in college rejection letters is part of a little game that's being played.

Cultivating a home life and family culture that's as stress-free as possible will make a difference.

The job market is rapidly changing, and counterintuitively, it's a slower-paced childhood that will prepare kids for it.

Instead of racing through the twists and turns and obstacles of a race we don't need to be in, we can confidently change our pace to a leisurely stroll. We can let go of our endless worry, our immense exhaustion, our staggering burdens, and just be together, knowing that this is not only enough but also what is needed. Living fully today is what prepares us for tomorrow, and what that looks like for our families and our children is up to us.

Discussion Questions

1. What does your weekly calendar look like? How much margin do you have in your life?
2. What were some of your favorite games to play as a kid? What are some of your favorite games now?
3. Would you consider yourself right-brained or left-brained? How does that affect your life?

Action and Adventure Prompts

1. Determine the dominances of your family members. Talk through what might happen to your learning and functioning in stressful situations.
2. Learn something new on your own timeline that you've always been interested in learning.
3. Host a family game night at a local park and invite others.

three

Rescue Childhood and Save Your Sanity

What Play Unlocks

I wish I had not been in such a hurry to get on to the next thing: dinner, bath, book, bed. I wish I had treasured the doing a little more and the getting it done a little less.

Anna Quindlen

Welcome to today. Maybe you hardly slept a wink last night—an ongoing pattern. The baby just spit up on today's outfits, yours and his. Plus, it's on the floor. The other kids are hungry and now they're fighting. You're behind on several text threads. There's a looming work deadline, the laundry needs switched over, you're out of milk. There's a lovely chorus of crying and fussing as your backdrop music. It's a wonder that you're even holding this book! Possibly you've read this paragraph more than once, which is how I tend to read books since becoming a parent.

Understanding some of the changes from generation to generation is all well and good, but we need help now—today. What will help right now as I am crumpling under the weight of the tasks, the immediacies of the needs, and the expectations of others? One answer—might I daresay *the* answer—connects us to the generations gone by and empowers us in this exact moment, while at the same time sets up our entire family for a brighter future.

There are lots of other answers with strings attached: Screens that turn kids into zombies and then raging maniacs. Avoidance that robs us of our limited years with our children. Substances that numb it all away. But the answer to what helps us both now and later isn't a rob-Peter-to-pay-Paul type of solution. It's one that enhances just about everything. It's the rising tide that lifts all the boats, yours included.

This answer coincides with a new name I've been given over the last decade. I have one of those types of names that has a lot of possible nicknames. Named after my paternal grandmother, Virginia, I've always gone by Ginny, but there are so many other options, and I've tried to make a swap on a few different occasions. The choices range from Ginger to Ivy to Nini to Gigi to Nina to even Dingle (that last one is out for sure). Over the past decade, I've started to be called something else: "The 1000 Hours Outside Lady." Or, occasionally, if the person is struggling with their number sense, "The 100 Hours Outside Lady" or "The 10,000 Hours Outside Lady." I've responded to all three as we travel the country for conferences and family trips, and even as we're out and about around our hometown. People recognize my face, but often they recognize my voice first from listening to my podcast. "Are you the 1000 Hours Outside Lady?" is better than "Are you Dingle?"

There are many authors who travel to gain firsthand experience about the topic they are covering. In *The Comfort Crisis: Embrace Discomfort to Reclaim Your Wild, Happy, Healthy Self*, Michael Easter embarked on a thirty-three-day rugged hunting expedition in the Alaskan backcountry. Carrying a heavy pack, Easter traversed through the most grueling conditions and came out better for it in the end. *The Blue Zones: 9 Lessons for Living Longer from the People Who've Lived the Longest* took National Geographic explorer Dan Buettner all around the world in search of longevity secrets. Alastair Humphreys, National Geographic Adventurer of the Year, has cycled around the world, crossed Iceland by foot, and rowed across the Atlantic Ocean. He recounts many of his adventures in the fourteen books he has written to date.

After reading books like these and many others, I started to feel unworthy as I embarked on writing my own book. I possess everyday experiences, nothing notable. Here are some of my standout accomplishments: I've pushed a stroller to the local ice cream shop. I've sat on a park bench while our kids played in the sand volleyball court. I've spread out countless simple picnics on patches of flat grass. I've set up a water table on our small balcony when we didn't have our own yard. I've walked to the library and the nearby school playground. I've watched some remarkable Lake Michigan sunsets. I've visited pumpkin patches, picked apples, and petted goats. We have gone on a few family adventures outside the boundaries of our wonderful state, the "land of the hand," but those are the exception, not the rule.

I've not done much that seems momentous. There was no extensive travel required to write this book. Instead, just the faithful trudge of the day-to-day with an added intention of getting outside for around 1000 hours each year (though this would've seemed extremely significant to me at an earlier point in my mothering). My story—this story—comes out of those ordinary moments, as well as the ones chronicled by hundreds of thousands of kids around the world who, along with their families, are fiercely protecting essential parts of childhood and beyond.

At the outset, play seems so frivolous, strange even. I rarely step back to observe our kids in play. There's so much to accomplish on a day-to-day basis that if they become engrossed in building a structure out of blocks or having their plastic animal figurines converse with each other, I grab those minutes by the horn and frantically try to accomplish something—anything. I respond to the text message thread so I don't get booted from our friend group, fold a few shirts, prep dinner, clear out some cobwebs, write a paragraph or two. You never know how much time you're going to get when a child falls down the hole of imagination, and that can add to the anxiety of the day. Everything is so chaotic and unknown. Will I get fifteen minutes or forty-two? How long until I'm pulled from the task at hand to intervene, to soothe, to feed?

You have to be flexible to be a parent, which flies in the face of many of our upbringings that were structured and orderly. I spent thirteen years of my life dictated by bells that rang at predictable times and schedules that had little variance aside from the random field trips where I hated carrying around a clipboard. Thirteen years of a predictable framework. It prepared me for some things but not for the pandemonium of child-rearing. I spent the entirety of my first many years of parenting grasping for some semblance of control and attempting to force us all into a little more predictability. (Truthfully, I still do that.) It never worked. It still hasn't.

But there have been other times, mainly times when we are out of the house, where the cares of today are not so pressing. At the local park, I can't attend to or even see the pile of dishes in the sink. In those situations, time is present before us. It is laid out and stretched a little. In those moments we can sit back and observe.

My memories include a few standout observations of play, like the time our youngest was two and turned a mango into her baby. She pretended to buckle the mango into a car seat, determined to take her baby on some errands around town. She coddled that mango baby. She talked to her mango baby. She made plans for her baby to meet up with friends. She fed it and nurtured it and played with it in a variety of ways. I had a front-row seat. Probably someone ate the mango eventually, but for quite a while I marveled at my daughter's capacity to draw so much out of something so insignificant.

Our kids have made families out of small sticks and built forts and played mud kitchen, all with no promptings. These activities appear out of place given what will be required of them in less than two decades when they have graduated from their childhoods. Mango babies and stick families are a far cry from the harsh realities that seem to be waiting for them. Welcome to adulthood. Here's an unstable and rapidly changing job market.

As parents and caregivers, we've made choices that appear to be in the best interest of our kids. In an effort to provide the most secure path to success, we've become a society that fills up childhood. We stuff in opportunities like an overpacked suitcase. Can we fit just one more in? Maybe two? If we sit on the suitcase, it might still close. There is an abundance of experiences and toys that are touted as educational, and we're cautious (terrified?) of letting our kids miss out.

But play—the unstructured, mango-baby kind—brings the child to life and helps them develop autonomy, social skills, and innovation. According to Nicholas Kardaras, author of *Glow Kids*, being creative is "the most neurosynaptically difficult skill we can learn."[1]

I am far from being an extremely creative person. My brain tends toward the analytical. But the times when creativity strikes aren't when I'm engaged in a directed activity, where all the steps have been laid out before me. Innovation arrives in the blank spaces. If we are aiming to prepare our children for a future that we can't even fully grasp, it seems that flexibility and adaptation of thought should be top goals.

VTech touts itself as being the "global leader in educational toys," and they use the phrase "make learning playful" in their advertising.[2] But we will not be duped. We already know. We don't have to make learning into anything. Learning is inherently playful for children.

VTech's offerings currently include a gaming chair designed for "the Seriously Cute Gamer" (ages one and a half to four years). This 2022 Toy of the Year finalist advertises itself this way: "Sit and play in an interactive game station with a swivel seat, joystick and pretend headphones. Little ones can game on just like the big kids, but without the worry of Wi-Fi."[3]

Wi-Fi is the least of what concerns me with this toy. Just about every toy VTech sells has a trademarked name with touch pads and sounds. Each ad ends with a requirement for batteries, a further investment into an already pricey toy market. These toys are made with a "planned obsolescence," as Dr. Susan Linn describes it.[4] When the initial elation eventually gives way to the doldrums, it's the toy manufacturers that win.

We were made to create, to use our hands and our minds and pull beauty out of the depths of our souls. Children are no different. They are driven to push and pull and squish and pinch and twist and press and build. These electronic toys, as clever as they may be named, don't adequately capture the innateness of a child, so they conveniently lose their luster just in time for the next round of Toy of the Year. There are no mango babies listed anywhere on toy sites because there's no money in that. There's not a dime of profit to be found in the glorious imagination of a child because they can turn anything into something substantial.

And yet, the wording of marketers gives us something to be concerned about. We probably need the Get Ready for School Desk, don't we? The insinuation is that children ages two through five exist for the purpose of getting ready for school. What if that's not why they exist? Why can't kids simply be those ages and enjoy those specific developmental periods as they are? What if simply being a two-year-old or a three-year-old and doing the things that kids do at those ages will get them ready enough for school? There is a strong marketing component that garnishes dollars out of fear and uncertainty.

LeapFrog is a subsidiary of VTech, and they have an online LeapFrog Academy for ages three to six. It's an academy? As in "a place of study or training in a special field" or "a society or institution of distinguished scholars and artists or scientists that aims to promote and maintain standards in its particular field"?[5] In less than a century we've gone from Tinkertoys, which were based off observing children creating endless formations with sticks, pencils, and old thread spools, to My First Kidi Smartwatch, made for ages three to five. "Kids will love taking these digital doggies on all their adventures while learning a little responsibility along the way. This super-talented pup can even be taught to do twenty tricks and will celebrate with barks and confetti."[6] What? The "super-talented pup" isn't even real. And all the bells and whistles (aka barks and confetti) are hard to ignore. As Dr. Susan Linn teaches us, "It's a protective instinct for our eyes to be drawn to light and rapid movement."[7]

The seeming convenience of these toys costs more than the money for the product and the batteries. They are costing some of the opportunities that are necessary for drawing out the inner resources of children. They are teaching kids to be entertained instead of looking deep inside themselves for sources of amusement.

The age we're living in, one replete with electronic learning toys, sends a message. VTech made 920 million dollars through toy sales in 2019.[8] That means a lot of people are buying these toys. Our neighbors. Our kids' classmates. So we start to second-guess. Maybe our old thread spools aren't good enough anymore. Maybe the type of play that costs us nothing is no longer worthy in the digital age. Maybe our child needs an electronic superpup instead of a patch of grass and a pile of dirt. And we fret because we deeply care. There's a lot at stake, and we don't want to get it wrong.

Carting kids around from planned activity to planned activity takes some of the uncomfortable guesswork out of parenting. It removes the awkward silences that accompany preteens. It pushes the unpredictable toddler off onto another adult. It excises the word "boredom" from the family lexicon. It allows us to enter into conversations with other parents about the extracurriculars our kids are involved in this year instead of being an outsider. But in this way, we all seem to become cogs in a machine, without the thrill of the unknown and the unplanned. Even if it's just to prepare our kids for their own parenting, childhood should include some disarray. It seems a bit unfair to craft a neat and tidy formative experience only to unleash our children into a world that is anything but.

In a world where most of us feel overworked, overburdened, and worn out, respite is available now, and it's in a place society rarely deems worthy to look: child-directed play.

Simple play prepares children. It prepares them for all those unknowns that lie ahead in the hazy future. When nothing but time is spread before a child, they experience gains in executive cognitive function, social skills, and emotional well-being.

These wide expanses of life seem daunting at first, but we can find life there too. No longer resigned to chauffeur, we can join in the play. Or we can sit along the periphery, engaging in something that brings us to life—a quick workout, a knitting project, a conversation with a close friend, a thrilling plotline of a book. Our child's space becomes our space too in a world that never seems to slow down. And the better adept our child becomes at play, which is a skill just like anything else, the longer stretches of reprieve we have as parents to finish pressing tasks or simply delight in life.

In a well-intentioned effort to prepare children for what lies ahead, we've narrowed our focus to the school desk. Literacy is a prime example of how we've shifted our approach. Over the course of twenty years, we've moved from 31 percent to 80 percent of teachers expecting kids to know how to read when entering kindergarten.[9] Despite this increased emphasis and focus on reading, our literacy rates are lower today than they were 250 years ago. It's as though we're trying to force a relationship that just isn't right, in which one party isn't quite ready to take things to the next level, yet the other side keeps pushing and pushing, oblivious to the signs all around saying this isn't working.

I'm Not the Entertainer

In my early twenties, I taught in the public school system. I started with junior high social studies and then ended in my sweet spot: teaching high school mathematics for several years. I loved the students, but every day I felt like a circus clown. Entertainment was the name of the game. My students sat in teams of four. Class time was filled with lectures and learning games. It was a maximum-output situation because it was so easy for a classroom crowded with teenagers to derail. Our time together was planned down to the minute. Freedom meant chaos. Structure led to success, at least in terms of managing a classroom.

It's tempting to take the same approach with our time at home. Who willingly wants chaos when the opportunity is there to control? We can shuttle and shuffle from one thing to the next, and then it's bath time and bedtime, leaving no space for sibling squabbles or pouts of boredom. Sign me up for the path of least resistance.

But it's not just our kids who lose out when they're enrolled in the adult-directed path. We do as well. Our brains are wired for novelty. The well-worn paths keep us in a rut, but it doesn't take much extra time or energy for us to step out of it. We don't have to row a boat across the Atlantic Ocean or hike through the bitter cold temperatures of Alaska. Instead, we can do something much less adventurous but still meaningful. We can playground hop, going from one playground to the next throughout the course of an afternoon or on the weekend. Armed with water bottles and a few granola bars, we can enhance the lives of both our children and ourselves in a way that is open-ended and filled with possibilities.

When every single day is the same—packed lunch, school bus, piano lessons, gymnastics, dinner, homework, bath, and bed—life starts to fly by. It's the novel experiences that stick in our memories and cause time expansion for the moment. My family has experienced this time and time again. We do a little weekend adventuring to new places (or repeat places but in a new season), and our kids will remark that one day felt like several; a few days felt like a week. Routine activities seem to pass quickly, but the new ones enlarge time itself.

As we seek to insert the out-of-the-ordinary into our ordinary every day, we will be slowing down those hands of time that seem to move ever faster as we age. If it's the new and different that enlarge our sense of time, it makes sense why life seems to be flying by. As a society, we're inside, missing even the glorious changes of the season.

I don't have the energy or the desire to be the daily entertainer. But I also don't want to be the constant chauffeur, witnessing the same doldrums day after day. Thankfully, I don't have to do either. The solution is under the big blue sky.

Nature Allows Us to Deal with Individual Differences

Two of our daughters seem to be twins, though they were born at different times almost seven years apart. They received carbon copies of their gene pools. You can barely distinguish between them in their childhood pictures, and they have all the same interests. The older one, when she was four, told me that when I die, she is going to take all the guitars our family owns. The younger one, when she was four, would walk around the house with a ukulele. The song she

77

plucked out and sang was "Winnie Likes to Play Ukulele" on a repeating loop. They both constantly ask, "When can I go metal detecting with Papa?," and they're the ones who are vigorously searching for lost coins under vending machines and near grocery store checkout aisles. Even now, with seven years' difference in age, they like the same type of clothes and prefer similar styles.

If only all our children were like this. How much easier would it be?

As mentioned before, there are thirty-two possible dominance profiles alone, not to mention the Myers-Briggs personality test, the Enneagram numbers, the theory of multiple intelligences, and the five love languages. Even just knowing one child is a monumental task.

In *Ungifted*, Scott Barry Kaufman says, "Individual differences collide with limited resources."[10] In the culture we live in, where friends and family are often spread apart by considerable distance, we lack support structures needed to increase the margin and resources we have. Parenting is a scramble from dawn to dusk and often through the middle of the night as well. I remember the first time I heard the phrase "nighttime parenting." That's a thing too? It sure is! And it lasted longer than I could've imagined. Is there ever a break?

Somehow, some way, nature is able to come alongside each of us at our unique stages of development. For the infant, the light plays with everything we see, making even the same outdoor spaces around us new again. Sunlight streams through the trees, dances off the ground, and shimmers in the snow and across the water. We see things differently depending on moving cloud cover, and nature provides a symphony of surround sound.

When our kids were small, we brought a large picnic blanket along on every adventure so that the babies could sprawl out and observe. As they grew, they would crawl to the edge and begin to explore the textures of the grass and the feel of a knobby stick. A squirrel darting up a tree or a chickadee flying by would catch their attention. These were exciting months when we got to watch what a brand-new world looks like to a young child. These were also months when we had to be vigilant for choking hazards, and that could be stressful. But when we got to the point where we started to wonder if that stage would ever end for each of our kids, it finally did, and we could let our guard down a little.

Toddlers and preschoolers find an endless array of sensory experiences in nature, and all the mud and dirt is therapeutic for them, teaching them to create but also laying the groundwork for challenges. These early contacts with gritty gravel and gooey muck, whipping winds and buzzing bugs, help them learn to deal with small bouts of adversity.

During middle childhood, ages six to twelve, nature gifts the ultimate playground. Long vines become swings, low branches become climbing apparatuses, and the abundance of materials is a springboard for imaginative play. In our 1000 Hours Outside Official Facebook Group, people often comment that they took their child to a local playground, but the child instead found more engagement in the green spaces along the periphery. Nature captures them, draws them in, and engages with them at a deep and meaningful level, providing a place to learn, grow, and even heal through play.

Nature is needed evermore in the teen years when pressures mount and jobs, sports, screens, and schoolwork threaten to take control of every waking minute. These are the years when kids specialize and learn what makes them come alive. Do they like the challenge of mountain biking, the blank spaces of fishing, or the slice of an oar through the water on a river or lake? Do they like reading in a hammock, seeing a late-night crackling fire dancing into the sky, or having breakfast on the porch? Are they drawn to low-thrill or high-thrill fun?

Throughout our lives, nature provides respite. Give teens a chance to recharge, and we help them lay a foundation of hobbies and pastimes they can turn to as well as places they can roam when they come up against the hard edges of life. Jon Acuff refers to these as "turn-down techniques."[11] When our lives suddenly turn up a few notches and we find ourselves in situations that are hard to bear, we need a known set of activities and remedies that can help turn down the dial. For some, it might be a quick stroll around the block. For others, it's putting bare feet in the grass and feeling the warmth of the sun on the shoulders. Maybe it's a plunge into chilly waters or a card game at a picnic table.

Whatever these "turn-down techniques" might be, the teen years are the perfect time to learn them. Teens are going to need them throughout adolescence anyway, and then the techniques are also stowed away and ready for the remainder of life. Acuff even recommends making a list of them and sharing it with friends and family. Sometimes we need someone else to step in and guide us to what is desperately needed in a high-pressure society.

At all of these stages and throughout adulthood, nature provides the perfect location for building friendships. Of all the benefits—and there are so many—it's the relationships that have been forged on the insignificant trails of the metro Detroit area that top the chart for me. We have a small but tight-knit community, family friends we've adventured with for over a decade. We call them our "framily." It's not been the big, splashy types of quests that have forged these relationships. It's been the flat hikes, visits to nature centers, and picnic lunches week after week, month after month, year after year.

In the years when your house is destroyed (the old adage of "cleaning your house with a toddler is like brushing your teeth while eating Oreos" applies here), meet up at the park. You eliminate the issues of fighting over toys, you give kids more space to spread out, and everyone gets the calming benefits of the sights, sounds, smells, and textures that nature freely doles out.

In *The Grace-Filled Homestead*, Lana Stenner relates these early relationships to hens. During the day, the hens spread out, strut around, and enjoy their free-range living, but when the sun goes down, life in the coop tells a different story with pecking orders and squabbles.[12] Indoor playdates, especially with young children, are filled with refereeing. We're already at our limits, so who wants to do that? Meet up outside and let everyone strut their stuff. Provide space to spread out and explore, and you as a parent or caregiver will get that break you so desperately need.

For young children, the location you choose matters tremendously. If at all possible, find a space away from traffic. It might be a playground that's surrounded by good fencing or a large grassy area that is bounded in by tall trees. For certain ages, you might even bring a rope or some small flags to visually show kids their boundaries. Any adventures, whether elaborate or simple, that you have with another family or two build a solid network of friendships for everyone to enjoy, and these relationships affect the quality of your life and even the length of your life!

Loneliness, beyond the immediate implications, considerably increases your future risk of dying. In *The Comfort Crisis*, Michael Easter writes, "No matter how old you are or how much money you have, being lonely increases your risk of dying in the next seven years by 26%. Overall, it can shorten life by 15 years."[13]

You don't need much to ward off this epidemic of loneliness. A few texts of invitation can go a long way. Others are as desperate for community as you are. You don't need a large group—just one or two additional families will suffice. Adventuring as a group provides safety in numbers, provides friends to converse and commiserate with, and provides children with multiage play experiences.

We're limited. We're lacking. We're busy. We're overwhelmed. And yet we have these beautiful children, each unique in a way that will never again be replicated. Nature increases our resources to parent them in a worthy way, all the while enhancing our own life's journey.

Be the Odd One

I spoke at a conference in 2022 where a majority of the attendees had "a look." It's a look that is cool and hip as well as timeless—an interesting cross. I can't accurately describe it, but what I do know emphatically is that I don't have it. So I felt self-conscious. I tried to emulate the look. I tried to pick apart the pieces—the ruffles, the fabrics, the accessories—and figure out the nuance of it all. And maybe I did, but I'll never know because the dress I chose didn't fit and I didn't leave myself enough time to try something else. So I grabbed an alternative out of my closet, making the concession in my mind that it was close enough.

As the conference drew to a close, my family popped in to see the tail end of it and to help with tearing down the booth I had been sharing with a dear friend of mine. Her teenage son walked in and exclaimed, "Everyone here looks like my mom!" She had the look.

Then my teenage son chimed in. "Mom, we saw you from the balcony, and at first we thought you were a wizard."

I was mortified. And then I laughed until I cried.

Some of us seamlessly fit in, and some of us (or maybe just me) look like wizards. Well, what can you do? It's the nature of life. Though I originally so desperately wanted to look the part, I have laughed so hard about my mythical appearance that I'm glad in retrospect that my copycat dress didn't fit.

Life is a series of collecting ideas about how to fit in, how to manage our time, how to structure our families, how to grow. These ideas used to come from less assertive forces and in smaller doses, and we had time to try them on for size. What fits? What doesn't? Can we play around with this or that idea for a bit to determine whether we need to just adjust it or abandon it altogether?

Today ideas come like a never-ending torrent of rain. How do we differentiate between the good ideas, the bad ones, and the innocuous ones? Where do we find the time, amid our daily duties, to sort through an onslaught of information and advice?

In the depths of our souls, the answer is already calling out. It's been calling for a while.

Simple still works.

We know it, and it makes sense. Yet we've been enticed by the trappings of fast, of more, of stuffing it all in, of control. They've been sold to us. We've been marketed fear and uncertainty and then been given an answer by those same marketers. *If you will just do A, B, and C and buy X, Y, and Z, your kids will turn out. You will be fulfilled and happy.* But are we? We race from one activity to the next, swinging through the drive-through, eating meals out of wrappers, sitting in manicured fields, and waiting in lobby areas—each day one less than we had the day before.

I encourage you to be the oddball. Be a wizard with me. Be the one who follows your instincts even as everyone else is still shuffling around. Here's the thing about being the first to follow your intuition: others will come after you. You won't be the only one for long. Your influence will permeate. Others are looking for you to take the lead. Jon Acuff puts it this way: "Go first and give others the gift of going second."[14]

When I first started 1000 Hours Outside, people gave me strange looks. *1000 Hours Outside? That's almost three hours a day. Who has time for that?*

1000 Hours Outside? Who keeps track of their time outside? When I was a kid, we just played until the streetlights came on. Why would I color boxes on that sheet of paper? That's weird.

This happened for years.

Slowly the tides turned. All I was doing was sharing something that worked for us—something that worked tremendously well. It was a simple solution to an onslaught of problems. I chose to go first with a message of "It's okay." It's okay to do less. It's okay to slow down. It's okay to roll in the mud and skip rope and somersault down hills. It's okay to take your time, your life, and open up portions of them for your children to delight in their childhoods.

What is your intuition telling you? Follow it. Share it. What have you learned? What works for your family? Do it. Tell others.

Earlier this week, I got an email from a forest school asking permission to celebrate "1000 Hours Day." They had started the 1000 Hours Outside challenge with their kindergarten students, and by mid-November of first grade, these kids were going to hit the 1000 hours mark solely through time spent outdoors within the parameters of the school year. The 1000 Hours Day is a tradition they are starting this year and carrying on into the future. A whole generation of kids is learning to celebrate real life. They're learning that they don't need electronic superpups to find fulfillment. They're learning the joys of the deep relationships that form when they play together.

Our family was able to attend the celebration. What a full-circle moment! It was delightful. The principal asked me to briefly speak and then gave me a megaphone, but no one told me I had to press the button. So I held it right up to my mouth for the entire time, thinking it was on, but it wasn't. And then I told all those elementary school kids and their parents that I had five kids. "They are ages fourteen, thirteen, nine, and six," I yelled into the nonworking megaphone. Sorry, Charlie. I forgot the middle one.

None of what I venture out to do to share about our 1000 Hours Outside journey (or anything else, for that matter) turns out perfect. In fact, often I inadvertently embarrass myself. But our world needs our imperfections as much as it needs our prowess.

Many of the answers for your own life lie in de-stressing your kids' childhoods, but know that your impact penetrates further than your own family because others are looking for what you have. They are desperately searching for answers, for hope. They are collecting ideas, and they need these tenets of simplicity to be louder than the swirling voices of society. Pulling back works, and you are showing others that it works every time you head to the playground instead of to lessons after school, every time you put in the monumental effort for the weekend camping trip, every time you eat your meals under the sky.

You have the opportunity to step off the narrow path and run into the meadows. It will feel strange at first. You may be all alone, brave, and free, frolicking with your children among the wildflowers. Assuredly, others are coming. Guide them with your wizard's staff. Call to them with your megaphone.

We are a mighty and vibrant global community of guardians—the guardians of childhood and of future humanity.

Discussion Questions

1. What was one of your favorite childhood toys? How have toys seemed to change over the past several generations?
2. Is your day-to-day life overwhelming or manageable? What makes it that way?
3. Do cartoons derail your day, make it a bit easier, or do something in between?

Action and Adventure Prompts

1. Have a nature experience with someone who is a different age than you, and notice how nature seems to meet you where you are.
2. What might "Give others the gift of going second" look like in your life? Try it and see who you can encourage and inspire.
3. Set aside a day where you use only non-battery-operated toys, and observe how everyone plays.

four

Bored to Tears

Uncover the Gifts That Boredom Gives

Our society measures personal worth in terms of productivity, efficiency, and the maximizations of our potential. So we'd better get busy or we'll be good for nothing.

Rebecca Konyndyk DeYoung

We live in a society where the margins have been eaten up. There used to be boredom sprinkled about the day. In the mornings in the 1980s, I read the cereal box. Waiting for the bus to come, I stood. There were bus rides and boring classes and empty spaces where our minds could wander, and they were a mainstay of daily life solely because today's technology wasn't present to make it otherwise.

My intuition says that mind-wandering time could be and should be used more productively, but it turns out that our brains need time to sort things out. We cannot be constantly filling the bucket, so to speak. We have to turn the tap off sometimes and let things just be. Johann Hari says it this way in his book *Stolen Focus*: "The more you let your mind wander, the better you are at having organized personal goals, being creative, and making patient, long-term decisions." He makes the argument that mind wandering is not the opposite of paying attention. Instead, it is a different form of paying attention altogether, which he refers to as a form of thinking that is "crucial."[1]

As our technologies become more personalized to our individual preferences and life situations, it becomes increasingly difficult to step away, to set it all aside, to enter a space of nothingness like a wide-open prairie, where there is no worn path for us to follow. Knowing the benefits of boredom helps us choose it in a world that pushes for its obsolescence.

Steve Jobs never originally intended for the iPhone to be a computer in our pocket. With the smashing success of the iPod and the foray into digital music, which was considerably more convenient than CDs or Walkmans, there was a push to combine the ease of the iPod with a calling component, and it was a noble goal. Then we would have to carry around only one thing instead of two.

But as with many technologies, the iPhone and others like it steamrolled through society, rapidly gaining speed and functionality that fundamentally changed life before we even had a chance to step back and calculate the cost. We aren't forced, by nature of society, to endure tech-less car rides—or tech-less anything—anymore. In fact, the solutions to irritants and bouts of boredom are right at our fingertips. The allure of the screen is ever present because it's in our pocket or possibly right in our hand.

Our family is not anti-technology. Nothing brings out our primal instincts quite like being told we shouldn't be doing something we desperately need right now. Those whose children are lulled to sleep by the motion of a vehicle wouldn't understand the mound of stress that car screamers cause. While I understand that level of stress five times over, I may not relate to the situation you are in that leads you to use screens for your family.

In the early years especially, it often feels like there are no decisions, only desperations. Our first two kids are fifteen months apart. When we realized that was too hard, we increased the gap to seventeen months for our next child. Nope. We tried two years. Still difficult. Three? And then we quit. It was never seamless to add another soul to the mix, but one thing was for certain, when each new babe arrived, they looked exactly like the previous ones. It was like the days of old (or for those who still use checks) when you put a piece of carbon paper underneath another sheet of paper, and out came an exact replica of whatever you wrote.

I anticipated the birth of each child. What would they look like? Would they have hair? What color would their eyes be? Near the end of each pregnancy, there was a bubble of anticipation, an extended drumroll. Contractions. Body ripping apart. Ring of fire. And then, "Oh, you look just like the last one." We basically got our first child four times over. It was interesting to watch each of them shape into their own unique person over time, but in the initial days, they were more similar than they were different, including in temperament.

They all shared the common trait of screaming in the car—bloodcurdling screams. Other people's kids slept. "Your kids scream?" they would ask. "Car rides just lull mine to sleep." I silently seethed. It wasn't just the noise; these were screams of desperation. They meant something. Knowing that things were so wrong in their little worlds, and there wasn't anything I could do as their mama to soothe their aching hearts, was hard for all of us to endure.

So my husband and I fell into a decision, which was nothing more than a move of desperation. Because the mayhem lasted well into the first year of life for each of our kids, we turned to clementines. Little did we know it at the time, but our second child was a prodigy clementine peeler. While most kids master this skill around age two, she managed to get the hang of it sometime around her first birthday, and she loved to do it.

I'm not sure exactly when it happened, but at some point, there was a turbulent car ride where I happened to be sitting in the passenger seat with a bag of clementines, and in a moment of misery for all of us, I handed one back. Silence. The clementine became a saving grace. Mind you, our daughter didn't eat it. Peeling was her specialty, after which she would hand it back to me and a decision would have to be made: gift another or drown in screams.

I began to measure car rides in terms of clementines. A trip to the library—one clementine. Church—three clementines. All was well until we had to travel across town to see family for Thanksgiving. Would a bag of clementines suffice? How willing would we be to clean up an entire bag's worth of peelings from the floor of our vehicle on a chilly November day? Instead, we went to Walmart and bought car headrest TV monitors—and they changed our lives.

We've spent over ten years being outside for 1000 hours (or close to it) each year. We've also spent over ten years using screens in the car.

There are those who claim that car time is conversation time, but it doesn't seem to work in the van we drive unless the definition of conversation can be stretched to screaming "What did you say?" over and over. The physical distance between us and the decibels of the road noise compound, creating an environment with a whole lot of "I can't hear you."

We are a family who uses screens. Every once in a while, I do an about-face. I read *French Kids Eat Everything* by Karen Le Billon and attempted to nix snacking from our daily routine. "Hunger is the best seasoning," I repeated on a loop for seventy-two hours until I quit that. I also made a solid attempt at "car time is conversation time" and didn't even last an entire car ride before throwing in the towel on that idea. Since actual back-and-forth discussions were tricky, I doled out lots of other brilliant ideas. I dug deep into the depths of my own childhood. *Look out the window. Play the alphabet game with license plates or signs. Count how many holiday decorations you see.* I had so many workable solutions, but the kids came up with their own idea: *Sing as loud and obnoxiously as we can for as long as we possibly can. Use up all the breath in our lungs.*

Sigh. Here's the remote.

To a certain extent, most of us will sacrifice some amount of real living to a certain amount of virtual living over the course of a childhood. In many cases, that will serve an important purpose. What we are constantly battling is that fine line between cost and convenience. It's a decision, which frankly sometimes isn't even entirely ours, to determine how much life we are willing to give up to a two-dimensional, rectangular screen.

One of my favorite lines of a book is in Dr. Scott Sampson's *How to Raise a Wild Child*: "Nature is all around us, in backyards, schoolyards, gardens, and empty lots, relentlessly thrusting skyward through sidewalk cracks."[2] Life is that way too. It just needs a crack. A small space. A sliver. And life will triumphantly push through, adding much to our years.

My family lives in Michigan, and our long and dreary winters cause us to latch on to any remotely fair-weather days that pop up as we enter fall. In fact, earlier this week a two-day stretch of sunny and slightly warm weather sent us over to stunning Lake Michigan for a last romp through the cold sand. Nature sounds are soothing, and any chance we get to hear the wind, the waves, and the gulls restores our souls.

Except we forgot beach toys. We were out of the habit of tossing our mesh bag into our van, so we arrived empty-handed. Our friends forgot theirs too. We had already made the transition to winter parkas and wool socks. Buckets and shovels were out of mind. There was grumbling among the children, but there was nothing we could do about it. Lake Michigan towns become like ghost towns once school starts back up, so we were mostly alone on a long stretch of beach with no way to procure or borrow sandcastle-building materials.

A crack opened up—that small sliver of opportunity. The kids began to look at the beach a little differently, seeing the endless possibilities that lay strewn out before them. Drift-wood became small boats, and the kids scoured the area for pieces large and small that they could carry individually or as groups to add to their creations. A stump was rolled over for a captain's chair. The older kids used their hands to dig as large a hole as possible, one that ended up being waist deep by the time they were finished.

It was the crack, the mishap of the parents during packing up, that led to the creativity. Society used to be filled with cracks, times when cartoons weren't on the air and toys were less plentiful and attention grabbing. I don't think we have to fight really hard to get back much of what we have lost because kids have the ability to take those slivers and turn them into something worthwhile.

Maybe next time we should forget the beach toys on purpose.

We don't need an overhaul in the ways we are parenting. We just need slight adjustments. Bring fewer toys. Schedule screen-free time. Have a jar of popsicle sticks labeled with hands-on ideas. In *The Fun Habit*, Dr. Michael Rucker suggests having a "Fun File" with at least eight achievable ideas written in it that sound fun to you and that you could weave into your daily life.[3] Gather your family and have everyone create their own file. Playing board games, painting, playing music, dancing, baking, knitting, using sidewalk chalk, reading, and building homemade forts are just a few ideas. Recognize the benefits of having space in your days and weeks, and then guard those spaces with lock and key. Your kids will figure out the rest.

Boredom is a scary proposition because we are already at our wit's end. We are splintered off from family and from community and bear the brunt of burdens that were meant to be shouldered by many others. The joys were meant to be dispersed as well. A society in which children are sequestered misses out on daily sparks of joy, curiosity, and youthful energy.

Because screens are so dynamic and are engineered by the brightest, we've forgotten that the cure for wails of boredom can be small because children are creatively brilliant. This has, in fact, been proven.

In 1968, NASA was looking for a way to identify their most creative workers so that they would know who to pick out of their large set of employees to tackle the toughest problems. Dr. George Land and Beth Jarman were contracted to create a test that would accurately measure the qualities NASA was looking for. The test calculated the ability of a person to look at a problem and come up with innovative solutions, and it worked remarkably well to help NASA find who they were looking for.

Because the test was so simple, they decided to give it to a group of children who were around the age of five and were representative of the general population of the United States. Ninety-eight percent of the children fell into the genius category of imagination.

The five-year-olds were retested at age ten. In just five short years, 68 percent of them had lost their creative genius status. Another five years went by, and another 18 percent were out of the category. In a span of one decade, the level of innovative brilliance had dropped by a whopping 86 percent. Then the researchers tested over a million adults with an average age of thirty-one and found that just 2 percent would match the creative force of almost every five-year-old.[4]

Almost every single one of our kindergarteners is already a creative genius. We are selling each and every one of them short when we think we know better and we fill all their time. We are taking from them some of their potential. Where are their ample opportunities to let their creative genius shine?

We often look at childhood and believe that our age, our decades of life experience, give us the authority to dictate it all—to fill up the minutes and hours, to color-code the calendar, to turn childhood into something of a competition. Our child's classmate is enrolled in three extracurricular activities, so our child must be enrolled in four. We are sucking the wild imaginations from childhood, even as we don't stack up ourselves. Through our actions, we are stealing what we don't possess in a misguided pursuit of tomorrow.

Instead of orchestrating the lives of children down to the minuscule, maybe we should see if we are able to slide our own selves back into that 98 percent. What would it take?

And can we humbly realize that kids carry the advantage in some areas?

We are in hot pursuit of the things that will make for an exemplary résumé for college admission, completely forgetting that our kids already have them. They have the special sauce. They are the sought-after NASA employees. Their entire brains light up with fantasy, imagination, and wonderment. We are dimming the lights, siphoning their potential. We ask, "How can we make them like us?" when we should be asking, "How can we become more like them?" Is there any way to access that five-year-old we once were?

Our children will be on the hook for stepping into roles we've never heard of and solving problems we've never seen before. We must allow time for what is known as lateral or divergent thinking, the type of thinking that allows for many answers and many routes.

I substitute-taught for five-year-olds once, and only once, because it was exhausting in an indescribable way. The schedule was so rigid, planned to the smallest detail. Understandably, this was an attempt to make my experience as a substitute teacher of two dozen children I didn't know more cohesive. But I have found in both my teaching and my parenting years that the constraints we introduce that go against the very nature of the child make everything harder. There is an undeniable pushback that eventually gives way to apathy.

I recall my kindergarten year as one that was flush with wide-eyed opportunity. There was both space and time to roam, to tinker, and to use the full breadth of my senses. Why does kindergarten have to be the new first grade when it's the kindergartener level of genius that NASA is seeking?

All year long, we give lavish gifts for birthdays and holidays, wrapping treasures in pretty papers tied with bows.

Some gifts are long-lasting, and others quickly end up in the junk pile. Allowing for boredom is a lifelong gift that gives children the opportunity to turn nothing into something, into many things. Decades ago, parents weren't in the business of entertaining children, but these days, we've turned boredom into something scary that needs to be avoided at all costs.

A simple "No, we can't do screens right now" might be all you need to bridge the gap between the grumps and something extraordinarily wonderful. This matters. Sometimes all you need is a short phrase that you can use repeatedly and empathetically when the moaning begins. This is a strategy from the "love and logic" approach to parenting and teaching. Defuse the situation with "It's okay to be bored" or "I trust you'll find something to do." With your responses on a repeated loop and devoid of charged emotion, kids are going to lose interest and head off in pursuit of something to do.

If that method doesn't work, there are innumerable springboard ideas out there that can rapidly turn around feelings of dissatisfaction. Nature provides kids with workable materials that they can insert their imaginations into, falling into a world of driftwood boats on the high seas and corn-husk dolls that need a diaper change and a nap. In our 1000 Hours Outside Official Facebook Group, members post simple ideas daily: a pumpkin-washing station, magnet toys on the garage door, chalk paint. Sure, some families install zip lines or build fancy mud kitchens, but others give their child a pot and some kitchen utensils and marvel at how much fun they have in the dirt.

Boredom feels like failure, but surely it is not. It is the sliver that is missing, the springboard of all things fantasy and imagination. It is the entryway to a world of wonder. It is an opportunity to recover much of the life we have sacrificed to screens. It is our own path back to the land of creative genius where we all used to live.

Empty Distractions

In *Steal Like an Artist: 10 Things Nobody Told You about Being Creative*, Austin Kleon applauds periods of blank space. "Creative people need time to just sit around and do nothing," he reminds us.[5] But even if you don't consider yourself a creative person, the things he suggests—like washing dishes by hand, ironing shirts, staring at the same spot on a wall, and taking a long walk—give us a chance to clear our minds.

Cal Newport informs us, "Everyone benefits from regular doses of solitude." Everyone. You. Me. Our children. He calls solitude the "school of genius."[6] Even if we are physically by ourselves, we still have to nix the empty distractions—the chatter of the television, the flash of light from our phone announcing a new text or social media comment. Technically we may be alone, but practically we are always interconnected in a tangled web of people and businesses. Here's why this is crucial.

In *The Comfort Crisis*, Michael Easter talks about the benefits of walking—specifically the benefits of walking outdoors, and even more specifically the benefits of walking outdoors and carrying some weight on your back (also known as "rucking"). "A 20-minute stroll can cause profound changes in the neurological structure of our brains," he says. Wow! Just twenty minutes? That's great! "This leaves us feeling calmer and with sharper and more productive, creative minds."[7] How incredible! A twenty-minute stroll is thus a fantastic investment of time.

This is not the end, however. There's a "but," and it goes like this: "But we found that people who use their cellphone on the walk saw none of these benefits."[8] None. Not one. No profound changes in the neurological structure of the brain, no increase in productivity, no feeling of calmness. The benefits of a twenty-minute stroll require tucking the phone away.

I've started to view my life through the lens of analog versus digital. We can go down a rabbit hole with what constitutes analog and what constitutes digital. There are analog clocks and digital clocks. We hear of converting analog music to digital, of digitizing. A key difference between the two is that analog information is carried in sine waves (insert math here): smooth waves that oscillate up and down, much like the waves at a shoreline. Digital information comes in square waves, like a string of impulses. If the waves of the ocean behaved like square waves, they would rise straight up and come straight back down, pushed up from the surface and then pulled back down again without that beautiful, continuous roll—without the swell. A graph of digital information reminds me of the Whac-A-Mole game. It's either up or it's down, and it's missing the in-between.

In my daily life, I'm not thinking of graphs or waves. Instead, I'm thinking of finding swaths of time where we step away completely from the electronic. Kleon writes of setting up two workspaces, an analog desk and a digital desk. The analog desk has a large variety of colored pens, papers, scissors, and more. I would imagine he even ditches the electric pencil sharpener and instead uses the kind that involves a twist of the wrist and lets off a scraping noise instead of a buzzing one. His digital desk is where his computer and presumably his electric pencil sharpener are. He writes, "When you start to lose steam, head back to the analog station and play."[9]

Surely you can play digitally. There are an untold number of online games, video games, and board games that no longer require an actual board that can be very entertaining. Recently, we got locked out of our vehicle and played the digital game Heads Up using a phone. A description of this game on the Apple store says it was created for the "app generation." The premise is that you hold your phone horizontally against your forehead and it displays a word for the other players to see. The other players use clues to help you guess the word, and if you get it correct, you tilt the phone forward and a new word pops up. If you need to pass, you tilt the phone up, which also causes a new word to appear. It's similar to the game Catch Phrase, which can now be purchased as an electronic version, but the original version was round and came with cardboard discs that contained the words to guess. There was a bar along the edge that you would hit every time you got a word correct, and there was a "hot potato" component that added to the frenzy and the fun.

Analog play is markedly different from digital play. It has more of that old-fashioned feel—hands-on and immersive in a whole-body way. It would be implausible for many of us to have two workstations for our kids, one analog and one digital, but the concept of allowing time for both is what matters. When we find our kids or ourselves staring at an empty screen with a blinking cursor, move away from it for a time. Break out the Legos. Grab a ream of paper and create. Rake leaves. Plunge your hands into some dirt. Play an instrument, running your fingers along the ivory keys of a piano or strumming your fingertips over the strings of a guitar. Walk on a trail. Stop and listen for the sounds of birds. Bake a cake from scratch. Host a dinner party. Find a place to be quiet.

Silence has all but escaped our world. When digital life becomes all-encompassing, remember that the wide world of analog still exists, inviting you to partake.

Outside of Your Routine Is Where You Extend Your Life

Transhumanism. Cryonics. These are ways in which humans are trying to extend mortal time on earth. Ray Kurzweil writes about transhumanism in his 650-page book *The Singularity Is Near: When Humans Transcend Biology.* "We are becoming cyborgs," he writes,[10] and he describes the "Human Body 2.0" and then the "Human Body 3.0," the later redesign coming sometime in the 2030s or 2040s. Cryonicists are trying to circumvent death through a deep freeze that gives us a second chance at life once we presumably thaw out from our frozen state like a chicken breast on a counter.

Though some may sign up for these modern technology ventures, I will not be joining in and am thus left with trying to stretch time in other ways via the limited design of my Human Body 1.0.

It was in Richard Louv's work where I first read about our conception of time as it relates to life's choices. He writes in *Last Child in the Woods*, "Unlike television, nature does not steal time; it amplifies it."[11]

I don't want my time stolen, I thought. *Sign me up for the amplification!* Yet there is the common adage "Time flies when you're having fun," and we've all sat through periods of time, maybe during a lecture of sorts, where time has seemed to drag on and on. The conclusion might be that when life's a bore, it seems longer. It stretches. But professor Michael Easter tells us otherwise. In *The Comfort Crisis*, he writes,

"Newness can even slow down our sense of time. Therefore, time seemed slower when we were kids. Everything was new then and we were constantly learning."[12]

This reminds me of games or tests that are timed or anything that is time related. It all seems to start out slow. *Tick. Tick. Tick.* Then as we're nearing the end, time marches faster. We cannot turn back the hands of time, but we are desperate to slow it down. Dr. Michael Rucker continues this line of thought when he explains in his book *The Fun Habit*, "We often encode common events as a single memory."[13]

Small variations to your daily rhythms and routines leave you with more memories, and the more memories you have, the more fulfilling your life will feel. This could be as simple as playing some games on your walks around the neighborhood. Roll a Hula-Hoop to each other as you stroll. Bring a basketball and bounce it back and forth. Have deep conversations. Tell silly stories.

We took our kids on a hike at Burgess Falls State Park in Tennessee and then two years later to the day went back to the same place for the same hike. We have gone on countless hikes with our family, but even for young ages, it's the novelty that leads to solidification of a memory. It wasn't just the location. It was the conversation as well. "Oh, I remember this place. This is where we learned to say our names backwards and we thought it was so funny."

Biomechanist Katy Bowman has practical ideas for families. On a podcast episode we recorded together, she talked about playing a hiking game called Hungry Bear. It's a game both kids and adults enjoy. While you're on a walk through the woods, the person who is "the bear" says something along the lines of "I'm getting hungry" and then does a countdown. In the span of a certain number of seconds, everyone else has to scatter and hide. When "the bear" turns around, anyone who is visible is "eaten."

Games like this often sound too simple on the surface to be meaningful, but we've played them. It's a scramble. You're scanning your surroundings. Where can you go? What will shield you? You have to be quick, and then you have to be still. *Shh.* Don't let the bear see you or hear you.

Katy also plays Hoops and Spears. She will roll a Hula-Hoop down a trail, and the kids will have to chase after it and try to throw a stick through it while it's rolling. In addition, she suggests not always driving the entire distance to the places you are headed. Park a mile from the library and walk the remainder of the way.

Depending on the ages and stages and other dynamics of your particular family, these exact ideas may or may not work, but catch the vision. A little bit of variability goes a long way.

Childhood once had a feeling of expanse, but no longer. We've stepped onto the fast train. But is it because we're having fun? Is time flying by because adulthood is such an incredible blast? Or could it be that time pushes on ever faster because all we do now is what we've always done? Same commute. Same work expectations. Same meal plans. Same sitcoms. Same snacks. Same scrolling. Same exercise routine. Same lawn mower angles across the grass. Insert a yearly cruise or family vacation, but overall, we are bland and unchanging, and life swiftly rushes by.

What a stark contrast to the child who, for many years of life, is constantly confronted with new things. The leaves change colors? Caterpillars transform into butterflies? Snow falls from the sky and lands on my eyelashes? Wombats poop in the shape of a cube, and grizzly bears eat moths, and rainbows adorn the sky after a good rain?

With slightly more effort and a little more intention, we can use the power of the new to slow down our sense of time with our families. Change is built into our world. Weather and seasons make each day slightly different from the last, if only we'd step out into them and look around for the changes. Nature challenges us because it is unpredictable. We cannot control it, and yet that is the very reason it holds so much power to enhance our lives.

We can add these subtle changes both outside and inside our homes. Including another family around the dinner table pulls us out of a nightly rut. Eating a meal over candlelight or around a campfire is delightfully different from fast food in the car. A nightly game of cards instead of a shuffle to the easy chair and the remote control may be slightly harder in the short term but offers an immeasurably richer life in the long term.

Screen time is not altogether bad, but it is removing us from something good. We must dig our heels in the sand and grab those hands of time, holding them as taut as possible through a relentless pursuit of good living that comes through newness and through learning.

Instead of "Less Phone," Try "More Boredom"

Much of life is how we present things, and to approach things from the aspect of denial can make things harder, simply put. When it comes to our own screens and those we use within our family culture, we may be terrified to let them go, even for short periods of time. These days our screens are almost always with us, like an addendum to the seventy-eight main organs we have in our bodies. Do you carry your phone around with you at home? Do you take it inside the gas station? Does it accompany you to the restroom? Like a childhood imaginary friend, our phone is always there at the ready, and to consider a lifestyle change that requires "less phone" or "less screens" may not stick.

Cal Newport writes, "The urgency we feel to always have a phone with us is exaggerated. To live permanently without these devices would be needlessly annoying, but to regularly spend a few hours away from them should give you no pause."[14] And yet it does.

Let's approach this from another angle. Let's reframe. Let's entice ourselves with something that holds a larger draw, which may look different for each of us. For me, it is the water that persuades and pulls: Floating in a kayak down the river. The sting of icy-cold water careening over the side of a cliff. The spray of ocean waves. The chill of hose water. In the heat of the summer, I walk to my garden, poring over the depths of the colors of the zinnias and peering up at the tall faces of the sunflowers. And I always come inside soaked because as I spray the water from the hose and provide a fresh drink for all that adorns our garden, I also spritz myself— just a little at first. It's so cold that it takes my breath away, but it hands me my soul in return. And then I spray a little more and a little more, until I am drenched and happy standing next to the most brilliant colors my eyes have ever beheld.

It's either that or scroll through Instagram, possibly ingesting the view of someone else's expansive garden. I don't necessarily want to give up Instagram (or whatever social media platform is most popular when you're reading this chapter), but more than that, I want to stand in the spray of my own garden hose. I want to chase the waterfalls. I want to stand along the shores of Lake Michigan and let the frigid water lap over my toes.

We must acknowledge that our time is a limited resource and that it takes less than we think to live a supremely satisfying life. This is less about restriction and more about elation. Instead of attempting to thwart the brilliant and filthy-rich tech gods who are engineering our phones in ways that rival drug dealers, let's instead live our lives to the fullest. Leisure gives way to abundance. The screens should only get our leftover time.

That sounds good, but how do we do it exactly? We must schedule in leisure, and then we must fiercely protect it. We may have to scramble a bit. Sliding small adventures into the nooks and crannies of our days doesn't come naturally when it's so easy to swipe our thumbs instead. We must come back to our guarded schedule again and again with staunch determination to uphold our deepest desires for a full life, for an unmissed childhood.

It's human nature to take the easy route and to conserve resources. The history of our species compels us to live this way. Yet passivity offers us very little. The reward of having nothing to do, of having time to slouch on the couch for hours of binge-watching, glints at us like a diamond in a creek bed. But escapism is a false hope. The rewards we seek in this manner rarely pan out. We squander opportunity after opportunity when we consistently return to consuming content rather than experiencing the grand payout of the kinds of activities that challenge us, lead us to in-depth social relationships, and help us become better people in the long term.

Henry David Thoreau is often credited with the words "Most men lead lives of quiet desperation and die with their song still inside them." What he actually wrote in his book *Walden* is "The mass of men lead lives of quiet desperation."[15] And the charge to bring forth our songs, whoever's idea that originally was, can happen for us and for our children only when we've set aside time for singing and silenced all the other noise.

Discussion Questions

1. Do you have times in your life when you get bored?
2. What did you do when you were bored as a kid?
3. If you had nothing to do for a period of time, how would you fill it if screens weren't an option?

Action and Adventure Prompts

1. Make a list of eight to twelve fun screen-free ideas that your family could turn to when they're bored.
2. Play a game in the car together.
3. Switch between an analog space and a digital space while you're working or doing homework.

five

Good Day, Sunshine

Light as a Guide for Our Bodies

From candle to oil lamp, oil lamp to gaslight, gaslight to electric light—his quest for a brighter light never ceases, he spares no pains to eradicate even the minutest shadow.

Jun'ichiro Tanizake

Well, we did it. We purchased a light meter. It reminds me of a tool a Ghostbuster might have used, and it measures the intensity of the light around you. Some days, I can be found extending the coiled cord and checking for ghosts—er, levels of light—in different areas in and around our home. It feels nerdy, but I'm owning it. I literally own it.

"Lux" is the word used for measuring the intensity of light illuminance. Based on candlelight, one lux is how much light a candle gives off from one meter away. Homes tend to have a lux level of around 150. Offices and grocery stores

are around 500 lux, and artists performing detailed drawing work may need lux levels between 1,500 and 2,000. On
a clear night, a full moon emits about one-tenth of one lux.
Indoors during the day when all our curtains and blinds
are wide open, or at night when the lights are on, our light
meter spits out numbers in the hundreds—500 or 600 at the
very most.

Chances are you may have had no idea of the lux level of
your living room, your bathroom, or your closest Costco
store. You've lived your entire life and haven't needed this
peculiar information. So why does it matter? Because when
we step outside, everything changes, and it does so dramatically. Even on the cloudiest days, we get lux readouts in the
thousands. When it's sunny, our light meter spits out numbers in the tens of thousands! And as you will learn in this
chapter, these numbers affect everything from your mood to
your sleep. The newer protocols for the treatment of Seasonal
Affective Disorder (SAD) call for thirty minutes of 10,000
lux–level exposure.[1] Our bodies respond in substantial ways
to the light we are exposed to.

An awareness of lux levels teaches us just how extraordinary and adaptable our eyes are. On a brilliantly sunny
day, lux levels can reach 100,000, but even when we're in the
dark, we're still able to see levels of 0.0001 lux, a number
that is one billion times smaller. Our eyes will never be able
to fully contend with nocturnal animals like the raccoon or
with crepuscular animals like the coyote, but when the lights
around us dim, the tiny circular and radial muscles in our
eyes relax to allow more light in.

I've been in restaurants at the time of the evening when
they dim the lights, presumably to produce a subtle mood
shift. Hello, romance! For a brief moment I can't see anything. But my eyes quickly adapt to an environment that

initially seemed extremely dark, and the lighting change becomes a distant memory.

We've also gone on some nighttime winter hikes in Michigan at the state parks. The DNR lines the trails with dim lamps and asks that you not use any type of flashlight but instead let your eyes adjust. In fact, the presence of a bright flashlight disrupts the experience for everyone. Don't succumb and turn it on or you're bound to get grumbled at. In the darkness, your eyes adjust, and your other senses ratchet up a notch. You'll notice new sounds and new smells wafting through the night air. All night long the nighttime noisemakers sing their songs. The crickets, katydids, and cicadas ring out in a nocturnal symphony underneath the cloak of darkness that protects them from predators. And your eyesight performs better than you thought it would.

Since we primarily associate brightness with vision (i.e., "When is it time to break out the sunglasses?"), I'd never given much thought to measuring the exact numerical lux before. My eyes seemed to do that for me already. Squint = too bright. Strain = I need more light. I've got this down. I'm a pro. But our bodies also come with their own internal light meters. Rather than looking like the Ghostbuster tool I purchased (from Relentless.com), our personal light meters are shaped like a pine cone (and not made from plastic). Exposure to natural light is vitally important for these internal meters to work. So how does the light get in there? Through our eyes! Are you catching where this is headed? All of a sudden, time outdoors appears less optional and more critical.

Each of us has a meter called the pineal gland. It's a pretty reddish-gray color roughly the size of a grain of rice. From birth to age two, the gland grows and then remains stable in that rice size for some people until around age twenty, but for others it begins to shrink around the onset of puberty.

Located at eye level near the center of the brain, the pineal gland lets in light and darkness, and it produces one of our most important hormones: melatonin. You can think of melatonin as the dark-light hormone because when darkness strikes, melatonin production begins, producing high levels until morning or until bright light hits your eyes, which causes melatonin production to stop. A daily habit of allowing for darkness as night falls and then stepping outside when dawn breaks is powerful and life-changing.

You can purchase synthetic melatonin to help you fall asleep at night, but the melatonin secreted by the pineal gland serves another purpose as well: it signals to the pituitary glands, adrenal glands, and reproductive organs to release their hormones. Light exposure affects hormone balances and even the onset of puberty! It's just another reason we should be getting our kids outside.

Learning what the pineal gland does in animals gives us a glimpse of what it might do for ourselves. Almost all vertebrates have one, except for the hagfish. The pineal gland affects things like migration habits, hibernation, growth regulation, and breeding schedules. In some species of amphibians, reptiles, and bony fish, the pineal gland is actually a physical third eye (called a parietal eye) located on the top of the head. Usually it's covered by skin and extremely hard to see, but if you look closely at the top of a bullfrog's head, you may be able to spot it. It's a small gray oval between its two regular eyes. (1000 Hours Outside Adventure Prompt: Go on a parietal eye hunt.)

To get a better sense of why this gland is important for our health and daily bodily rhythms, let's look at how latitude affects the size and presence of this gland in animals. Lizards that live in tropical regions tend not to have the external third eye. Seals and walruses don't have an external pineal, as no mammals do, but their glands are larger, suggesting that their responses to the daily and seasonal light changes are more imperative to their survival in their geographic locations.

Let's trace the route of the sunlight to our pineal gland. It travels there primarily through our eyes, which are the only visible parts of our central nervous system and are more intricate than anything humans have ever created. Just one of our eyes contains over a billion parts, twice as many as the most complex human invention—a space shuttle.

In utero, the optic nerve and the retina grow right out of the brain itself. Of the three billion messages that are relayed to the brain every single second, two billion of those come directly from the eyes.

We have had some tremendous guests on our *1000 Hours Outside Podcast*. One of my all-time favorite quotes comes from my interview in episode 15 with Dr. Jacob Liberman, who said,

> Seventy-five percent of the light goes to the chairman of the board of your brain, and that part of your brain, the hypothalamus, is the part of the brain that controls all your life-sustaining functions. It controls your nervous system, it controls your endocrine system, it's the major collecting station for information throughout the body. It collects your emotions. It is the initiator of our stress response. And that's where light goes. And then that portion of the brain interprets what Mother Nature is telling it, and then every cell in the body, at the same period of time, receives that message and then orchestrates its internal functions so that it is synchronized, or at one, or in harmony with Mother Nature.[2]

When it comes to our sleep and circadian rhythms, the light that enters our body through our eyes plays a critical role. Our retinas have photoreceptors called rods and cones that send electrical signals to our brains and are responsible for our vision. These rods help us adapt to the dark so that we can see throughout twilight and into the night (and take lantern hikes at local state parks). Since the rods are not sensitive to color, we see everything in varying shades of gray as day turns to night. The cones, of which there are far fewer (around six million cones versus one hundred million rods per eye), allow us to see color when light is present.

While the rods are all the same, cones come in three different varieties! About sixty-four percent of them can perceive red-light wavelengths, about 32 percent perceive green-light wavelengths, and the last 2 percent or so perceive blue-light wavelengths.[3] Our three-color visualization system (also known as trichromacy) is shared with other primates and some marsupials and allows us to see a spectrum of colors.

One percent of the world is said to be "tetrachromats," people who have a fourth kind of cone in their eyes. Trichromats have the ability to see approximately a million shades of color, but by having that fourth type of cone, tetrachromats can see an unbelievable one hundred million shades. Many fish as well as certain species of birds such as the zebra finch are tetrachromats.

On the other end of the spectrum, it is cone abnormalities that account for varying degrees of color blindness. Interestingly, more tetrachromats tend to be women, and more men tend to be color-blind. And you can round out your next dinner table discussion with this fact: most other mammals are dichromats and have only blue- and green-sensitive cones in their eyes.

It was long believed that there was one pathway from the eye to the brain that employed only the rods and the cones. But in 1923, medical geneticist Clyde E. Keeler was working with laboratory mice when he discovered that the rods and cones might not be the only light receptors in the retina. He found that blind mice were still responding to light.

Here we divert from the simple names of rods and cones to "intrinsically photosensitive retinal ganglion cells," or ipRGCs. Beyond the rods and cones, these are a third type of receptor in our eyes! The ipRGCs detect light and signal to our bodies the time of day as well as the time of year. These specialized cells are meant to give information about light to our bodies, and they function like our body's clock and weatherperson.

In times past, humans relied solely on their bodies to navigate daily and seasonal rhythms, but telling time as we do today dates back to sundials and the Babylonians. The Greeks advanced to mechanical clocks called clepsydras (translated "water thieves") that they powered by water. Hourglasses appeared in the 1400s. Wristwatches were invented in Germany by Peter Henlein in 1504, but no one actually wore a watch on their wrist until one hundred years later, when the French mathematician and philosopher Blaise Pascal attached his pocket watch to his wrist with a piece of string. Christiaan Huygens bumped up the accuracy of telling time when he brought forth the pendulum in 1656. Over one hundred years later, clockmaker Levi Hutchins added an extra gear to a clock, making it ring every day at 4:00 a.m., much to the dismay of his wife, Phoebe, the mother of their ten children.

It would take almost ninety years for anyone to improve upon Hutchins's initial alarm clock, but in 1876, Seth E. Thomas introduced a patented, mechanical windup alarm clock that could be set to times other than four in the morning. Battery-powered clocks came about in 1912, which freed time tellers from having to use weights or the windup method.

And all along, our bodies continued to operate on a powerful, biological clock.

Water, weights, and winding may have kept the artificial time ticking by, but it is light that resets the extraordinarily precise body clock inside each of us. We take our cues from the rising and setting of the sun but also from the gradual color shifts throughout the day.

Our Biological Clocks

In a world that has stepped away from nature's time schedule, we see more accidents caused by humans working in round-the-clock situations.[4] In the United States, the most serious commercial nuclear power plant accident happened in Pennsylvania at the Three Mile Island Nuclear Generating Station. It was between 4:00 a.m. and 6:00 a.m. when shift workers failed to recognize that there was a loss of coolant water, which eventually caused the reactor to almost melt down later on in the morning. The 1986 Chernobyl Nuclear Power Plant explosion was traced back to and officially acknowledged to have been caused by a range of human errors that also occurred in the middle of the night.

According to a study done by a committee of scientists following the 1986 annual meeting of the Association of Professional Sleep Societies, human performance failures "occur most often at times of day coincident with the temporal pattern of brain processes associated with sleep. It thus appears that the occurrence of a wide range of catastrophic phenomena are influenced by sleep-related processes in ways heretofore not fully appreciated."[5]

The temperatures of our body have a circadian rhythm and follow a pattern that looks like a wave. Waves are all around us in nature. The brilliant blue ones crash powerfully onto the seashores, but all day long we are also experiencing sound waves and light waves. If you were to track your body temperature every hour for a twenty-four-hour period, it would also look like a wave. The shape of the wave for each person is surprisingly similar, yet your wave may have peak (more energetic) and valley (more sleepy) times that are slightly shifted from those around you.

Shifted waves are more commonly referred to as the early bird and the night owl, though as we age, all of our temperature waves tend to slide forward. By age seventy, our internal clocks have shifted an average of an hour to ninety minutes earlier than when we were younger. I learned this when I took a vacation with my grandma. She woke up early even when she could've been sleeping in. No matter where the highs and lows of our particular sleep waves are, everyone experiences extreme sleepiness at the body's lowest temperature, also known as nadir. This occurs sometime between the hours of four and six in the morning.

Life can get a little tricky when our waves don't line up with those of our family members or of our school and work. A fun project would be to make temperature graphs for each member of your family. Get the thermometer ready and track it every hour. Maybe skip while you're actually sleeping and use the information above about nadir to fudge those numbers. See who lines up and who doesn't. Talk through the pros and cons of the shape of your wave.

We are not machines. We have inherent rhythms, much like the rhythms that run throughout the universe, and they become confused and out of sync when we miss the color cues of nature. Dr. John Ott conducted experiments showing that blocking certain portions of the color spectrum when growing plants could cause a host of issues, including the plants not blooming. It's tricks with light that allow chrysanthemums and poinsettias—both of which are considered "short-day plants," where the flowers appear only when daylight is twelve hours or less—to bloom right at the exact season. People as well as plants need properly balanced light.

Just as the sun rises from the east, so does the darkness, and the entirety of the day rolls through a pallet of colors and includes variations from the shadows. This is so unlike the static indoor environments we spend so much of our time in these days. In generations past, when kids walked or biked to school, had lengthy outdoor recesses dispersed throughout the day, and played outside after dinner until the streetlights came on, they would've had a better balance between the changing full-spectrum light outdoors and the fixed lights indoors.

The master clocks that guide the bodies of all living creatures are remarkable, yet they are also affected by the bright lights we use to extend both day and night. Consider the extraordinary path hundreds of thousands of monarch butterflies take from the northern US and southern Canada to the fir forests of Mexico each fall. This is made possible by a sophisticated circadian clock often referred to as a "sun compass" that resides in the antennae of the butterflies. Decreasing daylight signals that it's time to head south, and "one of the most spectacular natural phenomena in the world" ensues.[6]

One of the biggest challenges monarchs face—one that many other nocturnal and migratory animals and we as humans face as well—is too much concentrated light at night. For the nocturnal animals, the kind of light found in a parking lot or at a high school football field can make life more difficult. Parking lots often account for some of the brightest nighttime lights in a community, and at a time when the lots are relatively empty. For us, it's the indoor electric lights and all the light emitted from screens that we experience after dusk that mess with our biology.

If streetlights, house lights, office park lights, and parking lot lights all come on as the light from the sun diminishes, this life of constant light can disrupt the function of the monarch's circadian clock and upset the delicate time component of their navigation south. When this happens, they may wake up and begin flying when they should be resting. Additionally, since monarchs orient their direction with the time of year and position of the sun, these light disturbances may cause them to miss their path. Researchers have said that as much as a single work light at a construction site can seriously disrupt their migration. Night lighting also has a significant impact on bats, sea turtles, Atlantic salmon, owls, fireflies, mice, hummingbirds, and moths.

One of my husband's favorite jokes is about a moth. This particular moth goes into a podiatrist's office and immediately begins telling of all his family's troubles: the moth child that fell in the cold winter, the unhappy home life with his moth wife, the cowardice he feels at what a failure he is as a moth. The podiatrist says, "Moth, man, this is really serious stuff you're dealing with, but why did you come in here? I'm a podiatrist—you should be seeing a psychiatrist." The moth simply says, "Well, the light was on." Even though it's a silly dad joke, it makes the point that no matter what the circumstances are, moths simply cannot avoid being attracted to light.

Programs like the International Dark Sky Places promote "excellent stewardship of the night sky"[7] not only for the sake of the nocturnal and migratory animals but also for the sake of our children's children, who, at the rate at which we are expanding bright lights at night, will never get to see the Milky Way in all its grandeur.

It's not just the animals that are affected by the day-and-night cycle. There are many plants that also exhibit a circadian rhythm and open at regular time frames every day. Sharon Lovejoy writes the most endearing gardening books, and in *Sunflower Houses* she teaches of Linnaeus's flower clock, developed by Carl Linnaeus in 1748. Beginning at 3:00 a.m. with goatsbeard, each hour of the flower clock (which Linnaeus never actually built) showcases one or more flowers blooming. It moves from the morning glory to the marigold to the poppy as the day goes on. How fun would it be to learn to tell time by the unfolding of flowers and herbs?

When we allow ourselves to experience adequate time outside, especially throughout the day, our bodies will innately know when to start releasing melatonin—the hormone needed to help us feel sleepy. Writings from previous centuries show that darkness meant bedtime, as lighting candles was equivalent to burning money. In today's day and age of burning the candle at both ends and often participating in nighttime screen use, our bodies are getting mixed messages. With the glowing lights from our screens coupled with the lights in our home, we may never get our bodies into a place where we're flowing with the natural circadian rhythms of life.

Two hours of exposure to blue light in the evening will slow down or even stop the release of melatonin. If that screen use happens to be a video game, the combination of light from the screen and the dopamine secreted from an exhilarating game wakes us up. Television series are designed to keep us watching. Likes and comments on our social media posts do precisely the same thing since these platforms mimic human connection. No wonder today's youth are having such a hard time sleeping.

When it comes naturally from the sun, the blue-light part of the color spectrum is key to helping us wake up in the morning. That same light also helps with mood, alertness, memory, and attention spans. Dr. Chris Winter, author of *The Rested Child*, recommends having a bright, full-spectrum light near your baby's changing table, exposing them to that bright light first thing in the morning when they wake up.

Removing screens from the bookends of the day helps when we're feeling particularly out of whack, like right after the holidays or when we're in the middle of intense or prolonged stress. We can also make it a goal to see full-spectrum sunlight outdoors before we turn on a screen.

Our light meters are always working, but without daily light cues that follow the pattern of the sun, sometimes our bodies get so jumbled that we feel jet-lagged—even when we haven't stepped foot on a plane. Our circadian rhythms are just over twenty-four hours: 24.25 hours, to be precise. We need the cycle of sunrise to sunset and the black of night to keep our systems in sync with the twenty-four-hour day.

This can be a struggle for astronauts, who experience a sunrise and a sunset every hour and a half during their typical six-month stays at the International Space Station, resulting in a dozen sunrises and sunsets in one day. A top health problem for astronauts is their duration and quality of sleep due to this unnatural ninety-minute rhythm, which in turn affects their daytime performance. Within the last five years, NASA has implemented a circadian lighting system in space shuttles, designed to re-create the typical length of the sun's day-and-night cycle. Other companies are catching on to this need and creating products such as GoodDay and GoodNight bulbs, which send the right color wavelengths our bodies need to better differentiate between day and night. All of this is a glimpse into how we should be structuring our life, tuning in to the circadian lighting system that's all around us.

In March of 2020, when everything shut down in the part of the world where we reside, I was scrambling because I am the world's most mediocre mother. I'm just not all that good at it. I need a lot of help and support from the Costco food court and preplanned social outings where our kids talk to other people besides me. Those early months of the pandemic exposed my lack of skill and sent me on a hunt for new coping mechanisms. We flip-flopped our work-then-play daily routine that falls in line with conventional wisdom and instead started each day with outside play. For thirty days straight, we went outside before noon every morning. Some days, it was just for a short period of time—twenty or thirty minutes. Other days, we became engrossed in the emerging spring and stayed out for the rest of the morning and, occasionally, even the rest of the day. Besides, there was quite literally nothing else to do.

Work and then play is a common mantra, and many of us live our lives beginning with checking boxes and ending with a few moments of reprieve. Our family was no exception. Once we'd graduated from the infant and toddler years, we slated the mornings and early afternoons for work—be it schoolwork, chores, or the nine-to-five work-type things. Then we'd usually head into nature after completing it all.

When the world hit the pause button and we were looking for simple strategies to implement that would enhance our health and guard our moods throughout the uncertainty of change, we turned to the rhythm of light. This wasn't something I came up with out of the blue. Years prior, my midwife, Beth, had talked specifically about the impact of morning sunlight exposure, commenting in passing about how it would help our kids sleep better at night. I lost this nugget of wisdom amid the torrent of babies and toddlers, but when all our busyness screeched to a grinding halt, this concept resurfaced and I was reminded of how the simple daily practice of paying attention to the rhythm of sunlight enhances our days.

Some of the most well-run school classrooms incorporate daily and weekly rhythms as a best practice. Waldorf classrooms and Waldorf-inspired homeschools display their weekly rhythms, written beautifully with swirling watercolor paints. They might look something like the traditional English poem: "Wash on Monday. Bake on Tuesday. Mend on Wednesday. Churn on Thursday. Clean on Friday. Bake on Saturday. Rest on Sunday." Rhythms need to work for the unique needs of our families, but they can also provide a sense of security while the world changes around us. As Kim John Payne remarks in *Simplicity Parenting*, "Where well-established rhythms exist, there is much less parental verbiage, less effort, and fewer problems around transitions."[8]

Sunrise. Sunset. That beautiful refrain. And yet, how often do we miss it?

Our family lives a few hours from the stunning shores of Lake Michigan. The quaintest of towns line the ninety miles of coastline in our state from South Haven and St. Joseph in the south to Ludington and Frankfort in the north. We're just close enough to make a day trip out to some of these destinations, and we always aim to catch a breathtaking sunset after a day of sandcastle-building competitions and wave jumping. But not all days are conducive to watching the sun slowly disappear over the water. Though the world grows darker, so often clouds cover the action. Maybe we catch a few sunsets each summer that leave us in awe, but that's it.

We live amid rhythms. The tide comes in and goes out, in and out. The seasons change. The leaves fall, the world is blanketed in white, the crocuses pop up, our feet hit the sand. When we embrace the patterns that are naturally given to us, we find more ease in the rhythms of sleeping and waking. It's true for our kids, and it's true for us too.

Light Hunger

As winter fades into spring in our home state of Michigan, often with bits of melting snow and ice still blanketing the grass, you'll begin to see kids shedding their shoes and winter clothes. They'll lie in T-shirts and shorts on the hard cement ground, eyes closed, taking in the sunshine that has been hidden for so long. Their bodies know what they need. They are craving the full-spectrum light that only the sun gives.

Depending on your geographical location, there may be times of the year when it's much more difficult to get enough sunlight exposure. Norman E. Rosenthal, who studied the link between lack of light and depression, coined Seasonal Affective Disorder in 1984. SAD is especially prevalent in winter months and in geographic locations that get less sunlight.

When we had four kids under five, I entered the Olympic competition of getting young children dressed into winter gear. I didn't win, but at least I tried.

When the temperatures are bitterly cold and the wind bites our faces, a cozy blanket and a crackling indoor fire have the power of a magic spell. How could we possibly step out into the howling wind and the swirling snow? But when we set aside the arduous minutes needed to finagle little fingers into the little slots of their little gloves so we could head into the elements, knowing someone would have to pee momentarily, the sun's light still did something for our bodies. Though we were miserably cold, we also felt immeasurably better because that indoor lux just isn't bright enough to cut it—even if we weren't outside for very long at all.

On the flip side, if you live in an area with scorching summers, the lure of air-conditioning traps you in almost like a prisoner. How can you leave the cool of the indoors when it's sweltering outside? And unlike in frigid winters, when you can layer up in a tank top, T-shirt, long-sleeve tee, hoodie, and parka, you can only disrobe so much when the temperatures hit the triple digits. But if you can still manage to get outside, maybe in the early mornings or evenings when it isn't quite so hot, you will feed your light hunger with a dose of full-spectrum sunshine.

My journey as a mother was one of overwhelm until we began to allow nature in. What I have found over and over again in the great outdoors are simple solutions to modern-day problems. But just because the solutions are simple and easy to comprehend doesn't necessarily mean that they're easy to implement.

Michael Pollan, American author and journalist, sums up everything he's learned about health and food in seven words: "Eat food, not too much, mostly plants."[9] I've got him beat with six words: "Go outside, play outside, stay outside." If you could get your hands on a copy of the *Journal of the American Medical Association* from 1927, you'd find these words: "Light is to Health and Happiness as Darkness is to Disease and Despair."[10]

Even though society is advancing at an unprecedented pace and doesn't seem to be slowing down, our baseline needs to remain the same. We've lost our way regarding simple play experiences and our bodies' need for sunlight exposure.

In 450 BCE, people were using solariums, rooms surrounded by glass made to let in maximum sunlight. Herodotus, also known as the father of history, remarked, "Being exposed to the sun is highly recommended for those people who need to regain their health."[11] In stepping back toward this ancient wisdom, we are stepping forward for our own well-being during a time where the indoors and unnatural light are beckoning to us.

A Change in Light Source

We rarely think about light until a power outage sends us digging through a closet to find some candles, or until we've taken a weekend camping trip and the brightness of day begins fading into the deep purple hues of sunset. Campfire sparks fly overhead, and our bodies begin winding down as the light of day disappears over the horizon.

For most of my life, I thought of light only in terms of vision. A corner lamp allowed my eyes to match socks in the early morning or read into the late evening. If it was too bright outside during the day, I'd grab a pair of sunglasses or flip down the sun visor in our vehicle. I was unaware of the different aspects of light beyond how it affected my sight.

According to the Environmental Protection Agency, we'll spend only 7 percent of our entire lives outdoors,[12] which is equivalent to a half day per week. Some refer to this as chronic mal-illumination, a condition caused by living primarily in an environment without full-spectrum light.

Over the past century and a half, we've gradually shifted to getting the majority of our light from sources besides the sun. According to the Centers for Disease Control and Prevention, the average eight- to ten-year-old watches television for around four hours a day and is in front of a screened device for around six hours a day.[13] Eleven- to fourteen-year-olds sadly beat that number by three hours, coming in at a whopping nine hours a day on screens. Screen light decreases our blink rate by up to 50 percent,[14] and since smartphones launched in 1997, shortsightedness increased by a dramatic 35 percent.[15] Current projections show that about half the human population will be shortsighted by the year 2050—a number anticipated to grow 50 percent over the next decade.[16]

Children absorb more blue light than adults through screens. Considering school takes up a majority of the daytime hours, much of the time that kids are exposed to blue light–emitting screens is in the mornings or at night. Remember, it's the blue light that makes us more alert and has the potential to stop our melatonin production altogether. Light at the brightness level of a cell phone can affect sleep and cause wakefulness throughout the night. If kids are experiencing sleep troubles or sleep disturbances, this is a first place to look.

Incandescent light bulbs produce more red light than blue, and energy-efficient light bulbs hardly produce any blue light at all. Energy-efficient lights are primarily made up of orange and green light and were manufactured without any consideration for human health. So if we're looking for that morning jump start, inside is not where we're most likely to find the light signals needed to wake our bodies up. Knowing that the indoor light bulbs aren't giving us the cues, colors, and signals we need, we can adjust our schedules.

When we began intentionally spending time outdoors with our kids back in 2011, one of the first things I noticed was that they were sleeping better. Sleep quality affects the nervous system, cardiovascular system, endocrine system, and brain. A lot hinges on how our nights go, such as our focus, problem-solving skills, ability to fight off disease, and general well-being. It turns out we have more control over our sleep than I ever imagined. The photoreceptors in our eyes depend on us to deliver them the right signals at the right times. Being exposed to light during the day improves our sleep and our health in general.

As we've been on this journey of spending more time outside, I've learned that not all light is created equal. Indoor light is primarily for our vision, whereas full-spectrum sunlight is a guide for our physiology. We all feel better when we've experienced the daily rhythms of the sun arching over the sky. Even the rhythm of the darkness of night helps our bodies recalibrate.

Chronobiology refers to the science of our bodies' biological rhythms, which are controlled by the sun's cycle. Light itself is a wave with peaks and valleys of intensity. Natural rhythms are everywhere, and they can guide our bodies if we allow them to. By tuning ourselves in to natural rhythms of light, we can experience profound impacts on our families.

Unusual Light Exposure

We went on a camping trip once in Michigan's Upper Peninsula in the dead of winter. It wasn't long after the winter solstice, when our hemisphere is tilted the farthest from the sun, that we trudged in snowshoes to flatten out a patch of snow large enough to set up and stake a tent. The sleeping bag I used wasn't rated to the temperature I'd originally thought, and I lay awake all night shivering, miserable, and desperately waiting for the morning. I won't ever forget the chill. But I also won't ever forget the stars! The Upper Peninsula is sparsely populated, and with no artificial lights anywhere near our makeshift campsite, all we could see was a swirl of stars.

Exposure to light at night is unnatural to our bodies. Modern life includes twenty-four-hour access to light, but it would behoove us to follow the cycle of the sun and the moon at least occasionally.

Getting outdoors for a bit in the morning helps me feel happier and more hopeful. It increases my anticipation of what the day might hold. By the time night rolls around, especially if we limit our screen time after dinner and even turn off some of our household lights, that deep sense of tiredness arrives, making it easy to transition into a night of restful sleep. The same is true for our kids, and so our household is more peaceful as a whole when we can observe the earth's day-and-night cycle.

Our internal clocks resemble the waves of nature. Our brains keep time. Yet the patterns and pace of modern life often pull us far away from the life humans lived just over a century ago. Around the turn of the twentieth century, three out of every four people worked outside. By 1970, less than one in ten did. We've removed ourselves from experiencing the repeated refrains of the outdoors, instead living by the beeps of alarm clocks, the glow of screens, and the extended schedule electricity has handed us.

When we expose ourselves to the twenty-four-hour solar day, we allow our behaviors and our biological processes to sync with nature. According to Dr. Zane Kime, author of *Sunlight*, "A series of exposures to sunlight will produce decreases in resting heart rate, blood pressure, respiratory rate, blood sugar, lactic acid in the blood following exercise, and increases in energy, strength, endurance, tolerance to stress, and ability of the blood to absorb and carry oxygen."[17]

When we make room in our lives for play and move outside with it, our bodies can't help but participate in the rhythms they're naturally meant to sustain. Then the entire family benefits. Adding natural light to the rhythm of our days will help our kids' bodies function better. These are the rhythms we can turn to during stressful life circumstances—and we can see how a disconnect from them and more connection to technology is impacting how we function.

Major thunderstorms, the ones that knock out the neighborhood power grid, cause some inconveniences, but those hours (and sometimes days) provide a feeling of adventure—especially to kids. Living by the glow of candlelight, huddled together so you can see and interact, creates a magical environment. For the moment, to-do lists are cast aside, and there is time to just be. Just like short camping excursions, these minor blips in our schedule help our bodies to resynchronize with the natural rhythms of light. In fact, some even recommend a camping trip right before the school year begins as a body-clock reset.

Though it's obviously not realistic for many of us to permanently live by the glow of candlelight, we can sync our rhythms more closely to the natural world's. Even if we begin with small steps like exposure to natural light upon waking and putting away screens in the hours before bedtime, our families will experience the benefits in tangible ways. We can receive the invitation to wake with the sun in the morning, bask in the natural light during the day as we savor time outside, and quiet our minds as we wind down for night with the fading light. A good day of sunshine turns into a great night of rest for the entire family, setting the stage for life-giving rhythms and long-term health.

Discussion Questions

1. What have you noticed about your sleeping patterns when you're camping? If you've never been camping, how does getting outside for a large portion of the day seem to affect your nighttime sleep? Have you noticed similar trends with your children?
2. What type of outdoor job would be most enticing to you?
3. Did you walk to school when you were a child? Were there experiences woven into your childhood that allowed you to see the changing colors of the day?

Action and Adventure Prompts

1. Track your temperature wave.
2. Use a light meter and find the lux levels in different parts of your home as well as areas outside your home. There may be an app for your phone that makes this easy.
3. Give yourself the challenge of experiencing dark nights and light mornings and see how you feel after a few days.

six

There's a Lid for Every Pot

How Play Enhances Social Skills

> The primary predictor of success and happiness in life is our ability to get along with others.
>
> Kim John Payne

I met Julie at a homeschool water park field trip, although "met" is a bit of an exaggeration. The story we tell now is that we noticed each other. I noticed her because she had seven kids with her. They stood out in a fun and jovial way. And she noticed me because our youngest was still in that cute, clingy stage.

Not long after the water park, I attempted to organize a homeschool field trip. I scheduled it for a weekend so the entire family could join in. I made it intriguing—a hike to a secret beach we had found years prior. I was convinced this was going to be the most well-attended homeschool field trip in the history of homeschool field trips.

Two other families showed up.

One was a family we had been friends with for years. I assume they came out of pity. The other was Julie's family, who probably came for the same reason.

Our beginning happened that summer, in small increments. Shannan Martin, author of *Start with Hello*, calls these "thimble-size" interactions: "There's no relationship . . . or bonus-parentship that doesn't start somewhere thimble-size. A hello. A shared laugh. A quick helping hand. Viewed through the lens of enduring friendship, these aren't throwaway pleasantries. They are seeds."[1]

In the years that followed, Julie's family and mine have traveled together, hiked together, sat on park benches together, cried together, and been a part of each other's monumental moments—birthdays, engagements, and even anniversaries (which was sort of odd but also fine).

I love the expression "There's a lid for every pot." Your people are out there, friends for you and friends for your kids. I think the saying should be modified for accuracy, though. A better analogy when it comes to friendship might be "There's a lid for every leftovers container." In theory, it's true. But often the lids are lost. They got left somewhere. They fell behind the cupboard. Unless you're super organized (you already know I am not), leftovers lids are harder to manage than pot lids. Sometimes you can't find the one you're looking for, and you have to squeeze a nonmatching set together and try to make it work somehow.

That's a better depiction of relationships. They're hard. They're a lot of work. They're humiliating when your field trip is a bomb or when you serve pancakes to your gluten-free friend. Yet these moments of connection are the prime of life.

You share a story with every friend you have. There's a path to how you got here, and these are fun stories to tell. This is a conversation topic that comes up regularly in our social circles. Sometimes friendships stand the test of time while others are for a season, but no matter the length, our deepest relationships are with those we've had experiences with.

In my research for this book, I came across many books that deal with some sort of pursuit of happiness. Joy Marie Clarkson wrote *Aggressively Happy: A Realist's Guide to Believing in the Goodness of Life*. Dr. Jean Twenge penned *iGen: Why Today's Super-Connected Kids Are Growing Up Less Rebellious, More Tolerant, Less Happy—and Completely Unprepared for Adulthood—and What That Means for the Rest of Us*. There's *Rich Kids* by Tom Corley with the subtitle *How to Raise Our Children to Be Happy and Successful in Life*. And *The Happiness Trap: How to Stop Struggling and Start Living* by Russ Harris sits in my "to be read" (TBR) pile.

Kim John Payne summed up the pursuit of happiness in the opening of this chapter. Happiness and success primarily spring from "our ability to get along with others."[2] It's not GPA, test scores, report card comments, extracurricular involvement, sports, or any of the other general trappings of childhood. It's not the result of chore charts or allowance money or many of the other details that ebb and flow while raising children. It's not even technically about depth of relationship, though deep relationships would be a logical outcome when we've learned the nuances of getting along.

We are more or less born with our personalities; kids come how they come. Some are more intense than others. Some prefer their alone time, while others need immense social interaction. Some are naturally more helpful, some are savers, some are spenders, some are meticulous and organized. There are certainly things we can do to help correct a child and guide them to a more balanced approach—say, for the kid whose money burns a hole in their pocket—but for the most part, our inborn personality characteristics remain steady throughout life. We aren't going to turn an introverted kid into an extroverted one or vice versa, no matter how hard we try.

Social skills can be taught and practiced, more or less. This is the *How to Win Friends and Influence People* type of stuff. Dale Carnegie lays out the basics: Smile. Genuinely be interested in other people. Be a good listener. Use other people's names when you talk with them.[3] In our home, social-skills education includes acknowledgments of and participation in another person's celebratory days, like attending a baptism or helping with a bridal shower. There's a lot of input that parents, grandparents, and teachers can give on social skills, such as writing thank-you letters or helping kids learn to listen more than they talk.

But neither personality nor a set of teachable social skills really hits the heart of getting along, which is at the crux of the success and happiness we want for our children. Truly learning how to get along happens through the process of engaging with others—siblings, friends, those in our community, and beyond. We can teach our kids thank-you cards, happy birthday phone calls, and the proper tension for a handshake, but it isn't until they are shoulder to shoulder with another person that they have the opportunity to actually learn how to interact in a way that enhances life. A set of rules without the accompanying repetitive interactions with others falls short.

Over the last eleven years, I have spent well over 10,000 hours outdoors in spaces where there were multiple children without any toys. It's a lifestyle that we have gotten used to but still manages to stir something deep inside me when I take a step back and observe. If my friends are around on the outing, there's lots to talk about. Work, home projects, holiday plans, what's for dinner, struggles, joys, and the like. But what are the two-year-olds doing? And the six-year-olds? And the fifteen-year-olds? They are figuring out how to get along, often in a multiage way, without any toys or tools except those they come up with all on their own, using their imaginations.

In a school setting, children are able to seek out those with whom they have a natural connection, but when we engage outdoors with other families present or with a nature group, the kids are sort of stuck with a finite set of playmates to choose from. This mimics all of life, where we don't get to handpick our neighbors, coworkers, or clients. Sure, we get to choose who we will spend our Friday evenings with, but a large portion of our lives is spent around other people who have randomly landed in similar situations. We can begin when our children are very young to prepare them for their social interactions of the future.

When children play, they are intrinsically motivated to keep playing, as Dr. Peter Gray writes in *Free to Learn: Why Unleashing the Instinct to Play Will Make Our Children Happier, More Self-Reliant, and Better Students for Life*.[4] There's that "happier" word again! When I consider one of the most enchanting parts of childhood, I think about the times when our kids are engrossed in the joyous experiences of playing with others. It's the tears that are shed when playtime must wrap up and the child is deeply and genuinely distraught to move on that cause me to stop and think about what we lose when we grow older. When was the last time I was so engrossed in the clutches of life that my soul was grieved to have to end what I was doing? And how often does that happen? Instead, I am rarely taken in and enveloped in the things I love and enjoy because I've lost the ability to be in the moment and spend so much of my days thinking about what's next. Children have a lot to teach us about fulfilling lives.

From a practicality standpoint, childhood is the season of life when we need to capitalize on this instinct to interact, because so often as we age, our intrinsic motivation wanes to an extrinsic one. Kids attempt to get along because they love life and they love to play. We often attempt to get along for the sake of maintaining or advancing a position in the workplace or because we know we will be neighbors with someone for the long haul.

Childhood play is filled with the stuff of boardrooms. In all of play, but especially when the materials available are natural with no given form or purpose, kids must create something out of nothing. At two, three, and four years old—and all the way throughout childhood if given the chance—kids are given a complex problem, and they solve it together. It's the problem of "What are we going to do?" that comes up through the whole of life. And miraculously, even at young ages, they begin to sort it out. They develop a play scheme, asserting their wills while simultaneously learning they must compromise or the play will end. It sounds something like this:

"I want to play castle."

"But we already played castle yesterday. And you told me we would play restaurant today."

"But I want to play castle again because I made this crown out of dandelions and I'm going to be the queen."

"But you were already the queen, and I want to make ice cream cones and open a restaurant shop."

"Can we have a restaurant shop in the castle?"

"Maybe."

"But I still get to be the queen."

"Okay. Well, you can be the queen and order from the restaurant in the castle, and I will make the food and deliver it. You can help if you want. What's your favorite food?"

These are not the exact conversations of boardrooms, obviously, but the gist is similar. We all must learn to assert our wills enough to where we find value in the interaction, but not so much as to cause other people to leave. What a balancing act! This is a game where there isn't one set winner; there are many. The winners are the ones who don't quit. They are the ones who are able to work through the conflicts, the disagreements, and make the appropriate amount of concessions—not too few and not too many—so they all can continue to play. Play helps kids learn to trust, exert independence, cast vision for ideas, negotiate, compromise, and accept varying outcomes. These are the skills they will need for satisfaction in the present and for success in an ever-changing world.

Dr. Gray puts it this way: "Playing with other children, away from adults, is how children learn to make their own decisions, control their emotions and impulses, see from others' perspectives, negotiate differences with others, and make friends. In short, play is how children learn to take control of their lives."[5]

Playing with other children, away from adults, used to be a mainstay of the childhood years. In her book *iGen,*

Dr. Jean Twenge quotes a seventeen-year-old named Kevin, who says that his generation "lost interest in socializing in person—they don't have physical get-togethers, they just text together, and they can just stay at home." Others comment that many of the social interactions that they have had were "almost always supervised" or were "adult-run affairs."[6]

Lenore Skenazy, founder of Let Grow and author of *Free-Range Kids*, notes that it is fear that is leading parents to overschedule—fear of mediocrity, fear of injury, even fear of the "non-organic grape." "Woe to the child," she writes, "who develops a good pencil grip at age seven instead of four."[7] When you put it that way, we realize how silly we sound. Can the childhood timeline account for some variations? And furthermore, is that trade-off worth it? Skenazy writes of the "impossible obsession of our era: total safety and control of our children every second of every day."[8] That sounds nice on paper, but it's a complete disservice to our kids, who only get one childhood's worth of intrinsic motivation to learn the vast array of skills that help them learn how to get along with others.

I love Angela Hanscom's practical idea of having all-day playdates, which she talked about on my podcast. We've become a society of micromanagers and of efficiency. So many components of our lives end up next to a box that can be checked off. *Two-hour playdate on Thursday—check.* But can we open up our lives a little more? Can we open up our homes a little more? It's not easy. I'm slightly on edge every time our kids have friends over, and though I try to calm it down, my mind obsesses. Are they having a good time? Is my kid playing nice? Do they like the food I'm serving? Should I bring out more or less? How much should I interact? Do they even want me to interact? Would the other parents want me to interact? Do the kids like being here? Will they want to come back? What is wrong with me?

It would be easier on my clearly high levels of anxiety not to have other kids over. Or, when we do, to bound the time into a small chunk so I won't have to deal with so many looming questions. Instead, I stuff the feelings because over the course of many hours, kids learn how to structure their time together, and this is a valuable ability to master. When families know how to leave room for play that enhances social skills, everyone benefits.

Forming a Nature Group

My 1000 Hours Outside journey began hand in hand with other families, and it continues to be the same way after ten years. I get a lot of questions about how to handle kids who don't want to go outside, and I think the answer that almost always works is to invite friends along. This works especially well for teenagers. Some good snacks also help.

Your nature group does not have to be large. Don't discount the power of having just one other family to hit a trail with. Camaraderie adds variety to the everyday mix, making even a place you've visited many times feel fresh and new. In time, people may come and go for a variety of reasons, but it has worked well for our family to have a community of anywhere from six to ten families who place a value on nature time and are willing to use their time in a similar way.

What I have found is that when the group gets too large, you become almost like an event rather than a person, and others then pick and choose if they are going to attend your event that day. This can be tricky because there is less dependability, and often kids get upset if who they expected to show up doesn't. I think there is a time and place to open up gatherings and have a large invitee list, but for our everyday excursions, we learned that in the long run, sticking with those who were committed helps us all fare better.

There is a chance of rejection interlaced with inviting others to do things. Sometimes they will say no for reasons such as scheduling conflicts or illness. Other times they may not be your speed, or the kids don't click. I want to acknowledge that this is not easy. Forming relationships as adults, especially when there is a family in tow, proves to be much more difficult than it was as kids because there are a lot more variables. Namely, there are simply more humans who need to click in order for the relationships to work. But it sure is worth it to try.

Kids do not have to be the exact same ages in order to form strong bonds. Our middle daughter's closest friend is almost two years younger than her. In traditional settings, they might not have even known each other. But they are each other's go-to person. They dive deep into play together. They will be each other's childhood friend who is remembered long into adulthood. And they formed their bond through family experiences together in the natural world.

Aligning schedules is another piece to this puzzle and is part of the ebb and flow of those you spend time with over the course of raising children. The beautiful part about coming alongside another family and having hands-on, in-person get-togethers is that even if you eventually go your separate ways, you will still hold a deep connection for life. We've gone on to have different schedules from some of our closest friends in the toddler and preschool years, but even if we just cross paths (literally) a few times a year, the ties that bind us continue to hold strong.

Having a regular nature day each week is a foundational pillar you can fall back on, giving you and your family a much-needed sense of rhythm and predictability to your years. It gives you something to look forward to, a day in which you know you can deeply exhale and let the weight of the world slide off your shoulders. But don't discount flexibility. If you can find another family who has some similar open spaces in their calendar, look ahead and snag the nicest days of the week to get outside and play. We keep a small seasonal list of favorite places in our areas, and we try to knock them out each year. Fridays have been a long-standing nature club day for us (ours is oddly called "Carrot Day," and I highly recommend naming yours), but we've had some grand adventures on a whim during the in-betweens.

I want to move away from the how-tos for a moment because you will figure those out. They will be unique to you. When do you go, where do you go, what do you bring, how long do you stay? Do you share food or pack your own? These are all questions you get to answer, and the answers will ebb and flow throughout the different stages of childhood.

I speak all over the country about the benefits of getting kids outside, and at different times of the year I tend to have a new favorite benefit. In the depths of winter, when the air is frigid and the clouds hang low, when the landscape is white as far as I can see and my body craves the colors of summer, it is helpful to know that exposure to full-spectrum sunlight can take a gloomy mood and turn it around. When I feel I'm losing my grip on life, I remind myself that the play my kids partake in when I feel less available than I would like is preparing them for a life of creativity and adaptability.

But something that tops the list of benefits, no matter the season, is friendship. The novel experiences we have in the outdoors grip all our senses and stick to our memories. Our lives are filled with "Remember when . . . ?" and "What comes next?" There is an air of anticipation mixed with a blanket of gratitude.

When our middle daughter, Brooklyn, was two, we met a new set of friends through church. They had a two-year-old as well. In fact, these girls were almost birthday buddies, and they clicked immediately. It's hard to even imagine children so young forming such deep bonds, but they did. And even though our families have moved farther apart in location throughout the years, there is nothing like the days when we meet up, hit a trail or a nature center, or just catch up in the yard. And we always feast, trying to grab the best of what's seasonally available in our area.

These children, these companions, are not just companions that our kids needed; I've needed them too. Parenting is one of the most demanding things I've ever done, and there have been some dark days. In times of desperation, when I've needed practical help, a shoulder to sob on, or someone to give apt advice, I've gone to the friends I have lived countless hours with and have parented alongside for over a decade in some instances. They know me, and they know my kids.

Nature puts all of us on an even playing field. Even if we have managed to step away from hospitality expectations—embracing the whole messy-hospitality philosophy that it's better to gather imperfectly than not to gather at all because our homes aren't tidy enough or our prepared food isn't worthy enough—it can still be stressful having people over. The missed cobwebs shine. We should've lit a candle in the bathroom. Oh no, the food is a little burned. But when we're outdoors, the things of this world are tucked away for a time. Invisible. We can just be, without the nag of all the things we could've done, should've done, or should've done differently. Outside provides us with an indistractable place, especially if we leave our cell phones in a hard-to-reach spot. Its counterpart, the indoors, is not the same because no matter how tiny our homes are and how minimalist we've made our surroundings, there is always something that could be tended to. Our attention is split. Inadequacy is thrust in our faces. It's easier to get irritable. Though there are physical components as well, leaving our distractions behind is partially why when we step outside, whether it's for twenty minutes or six hours, a lot of our stress melts away. What an ideal environment to form bonds.

The natural playground that exists to provide our kids with thrilling risks and lovely sensory experiences is a gift. But the outdoors also provides us a place to connect in unique ways and form fast friendships as we forge ahead on the trails.

You have to be brave with your invitations. Some people will say no. But others will be so relieved that you asked. They've been waiting, and they needed you to make the first move. Hand in hand your kids will walk the trails, and hand in hand you will walk through life with the friends you've made, knowing that strong relationships are a key component to health and wellness.

A Loneliness Epidemic

In-person relationships are on the decline, and Dr. Jean Twenge writes in *iGen* that today's teens are lonelier than they ever have been since research began measuring loneliness in 1991. Beyond that, "As teens spent less time with their friends in person and more time on their phones, their life satisfaction dropped with astonishing speed."[9]

It is difficult, if not impossible, to imagine what type of teen each of us might be today. If I had grown up in the 2000s, I wonder if I would have had a smartphone. Would my parents have allowed it? Would I have begged and begged for one, even snuck one if their answer was "no"? Would I have been taken in by the trappings of social media? Would I have had my phone on me at all times, turning to it in times of boredom or awkwardness? And, most importantly, would it have enhanced my teen years? I'm not sure about all the specifics, but my gut instinct tells me "no," it wouldn't have. My adolescence would have been more challenging to navigate with a smartphone.

I'm thankful for the freedom I had and for the break from school social tensions that the afternoons and weekends brought. My childhood didn't feel tethered. There is an irony in the need for having a smartphone to fit in, and yet it is the very device that causes all of us, even adults, to feel left out. We see what everyone else is doing and know we weren't invited.

Furthermore, the boredom and empty pockets of time that used to spur us on to create or connect have been sucked into the rectangular abyss that holds the promise of gripping our attention and not letting go. The decline in teen mental health indicates that we have to guard some old-fashioned principles of living in order for teens to have better lives. The principle is simple, though the implementation takes some ingenuity: less virtual and more real. Twenge writes, "The results could not be clearer: teens who spend more time on screen activities are more likely to be unhappy, and those who spend more time on nonscreen activities are more likely to be happy. There's not a single exception: all screen activities are linked to less happiness, and all nonscreen activities are linked to more happiness."[10]

Five researchers set out to analyze studies from 1980 to 2014 and found that social isolation caused, on average, a 29 percent increase in likelihood of mortality, a 26 percent increase in loneliness, and a 32 percent increase in living alone.[11] Now is the time we must teach our children and teens that putting effort into relationships is worth the hassle. On the surface, online relationships give the appearance of real connection, and certainly they are easier to maintain. We can build e-relationships from the comfort of our own beds—no need to even put on deodorant. But we can also walk away from these relationships with the click of a button. Our kids are looking to us to see how we build our lives, and now is our chance to dive into the invitations, into the rejections, into the humility that comes from an imperfect home and an imperfect meal, and into the great and unknown rewards that lie on the other side.

I invited our nature group to a progressive dinner earlier this month, which is sort of an odd invitation because it involves others also opening their homes. There were thirty-six of us, including kids. Appetizers were at one home, the main dinner at another (ours), and dessert at still another home. We progressed from one house to the next, thus the name (though I've heard that others call it "safari supper," and I like that name better).

Here's the truth. It was a lot of work. It was tricky to figure out the timing. How do you heat up dinner when you are eating appetizers at another home? In the final hours before the dinner began and we were in total scramble mode, the questions started to flow within our family. "Whose idea was this?" I considered blaming my friends. But I was honest and took the fall, and amid everyone's disgust, I second-guessed myself. This was much more complicated than having a regular potluck dinner at one person's house. It involved three families instead of just one having to clean their homes. Even calling it "safari supper" wouldn't have taken the edge out of the annoyance that permeated our home.

It wasn't even that fun (sorry, friends). It was fine. It was something to do. It was memorable. Meagan made a mocha icebox cake, and Julie made a cheeseball in the shape of a pumpkin.

I would do it again. Because what else would we have done? Sat around and scrolled on our phones? Life is meant to be lived, and there are others waiting to live it with us. We are modeling to our kids to make the plans and do the work. Even if the results are a bit lackluster, there's still worth to it all.

If a progressive supper (recoined "aggressive supper" by one of the kids in our group) isn't your cup of tea, or if something like it is not even a possibility in your stage of life, finding or creating community needn't be that hard. Take walks in your neighborhood or city and wave to people. Talk to those who are out walking their dogs. Join a club like a walking club or a ruck club or a geology club. Latch on to a group that's already formed and help with the planning. Learn a new skill with someone else. Deliver some home-grown flowers to a few people who live in proximity. Share the abundance from your garden. Offer to help someone—it could be as simple as pushing a stroller for a portion of a trail.

Even the simple act of uninterrupted conversation can be a game changer when it comes to relationships. Andy Crouch writes about a lot of the nuances of conversation in his book *The Tech-Wise Family*, and we talked about this subject on a recent podcast episode. A few minutes into a conversation, topics tend to take a turn to more in-depth, more personal matters. It's at this point, where we've exhausted the surface material such as weather, sports, and the like, that we reach a crucial crossroads. Do we stick with it, or do we turn away? Interestingly, if we turn away once, it's not just a blip in the relationship-building process. An exit from the conversation in these crucial moments to glance at our phones because it's an easy out actually becomes an integral part of the communication. It announces that we're not here for the depth or the risk. Crouch puts it like this: "All true conversations, really, are risks, exercises in improvisation where we have to listen and respond without knowing, fully, what is coming next, even out of our own mouths."[12]

Our phones offer a way out. They offer a way out of boredom and an exit strategy for uncomfortable situations, and I think so often we've taken that exit door without knowing where it leads. Brooke Shannon, founder of Wait Until 8th, a nonprofit organization that empowers parents to "say yes to waiting for the smartphone,"[13] offers compelling reason after reason to delay handing our children access to the internet at all times. One reason to wait as long as humanly possible is because we've finally reached a place to better understand the pitfalls of the cursory glances that seem so innocuous.

If a child, teen, or adult always misses out on deeper relationships because a brief look toward a phone deeply communicates an underlying intention that isn't meant, then maybe it's best if we don't treat our phones like an appendage. Maybe it behooves our family not to supply these devices to our young children. If the exchange of information throughout the day is truly needed, we can choose an option that doesn't have the addictive qualities to it, a phone that isn't a phone/computer combo. Our smartphones are only smart in certain arenas. They do not carry their brilliance into the arena of human relationships.

Todd Wilson wrote an empowering book with a brilliantly intriguing title: *How to Choose Relationship When There's So Much to Do*. As I write these words, I'm playing a game of restaurant with our youngest daughter. She's standing here with a notepad and a pen, taking my order, which is the cutest thing since she doesn't know how to write yet.

"I'd like to order some spaghetti, please," I tell her.

"We don't have that," she says.

"Okay, an ice cream cone?"

"We don't have that either. We only have peppers and sausage."

"Well, then that sounds lovely. Peppers and sausage are my favorite meal. How did you know?"

(She leaves and returns with a plastic cup filled with plastic peppers and one plastic red sausage.)

"Delicious!"

This is not the ideal writing environment. I envision other writers in a cabin in the woods, where it's quiet except for the sounds of the birds and the squirrels and the rustling leaves. Interruptions are at a minimum. But Todd Wilson's words ring in my mind: "Don't miss relationship in the midst of it all."[14]

Beyond restaurant, Winnie has used this book-writing period to draw me pictures of things I enjoy. It began with "What's your favorite thing to do?" (play the piano) and has progressed to "What's your sixty-third favorite thing to do?" (play volleyball). I'm running out of ideas. She has asked me questions I've never been asked before.

I realize I'm doing all of this imperfectly. My attention is split. None of this is ideal, and yet it's okay. Maybe that's the trade-off we have to make sometimes in a world inundated with information, where our work follows us around like a loyal dog.

National Geographic explorer Alastair Humphreys writes of "microadventures," the small adventures that still give us the benefits of large adventures but are on a scale that fits within our harried lives. If we can't bike around the world, can we bike to the corner store with our kids and buy an ice cream cone? We will still get the feelings of freedom and novelty as the wind blows our hair and we reach our desired destination. One of the podcast episodes Alastair and I recorded together is called "Microadventures: Because Small Adventures Are Better Than None at All." Maybe we could say the same thing about this distracted age we live in—"Microinteractions: Because some interactions are better than none at all."

We all have things to do, things we are committed to. But I don't think it takes all that much to elevate our human relationships and keep them in their proper place. In *Being Your Best When Your Kids Are at Their Worst*, Kim John Payne writes of a business marketing expert and author, David Levin, who doesn't make sweeping changes when he isn't successful in business. Instead, he makes minor adjustments, "a tiny two-degree directional change."[15]

By many current measures, our social relationships are slipping through our fingers, and it's showing up in the quality of our lives. But we can tweak our way to where we want to go. Let's have nine-minute conversations with our phones safely tucked away in a bag or a drawer. Let's invite the neighbor kids over to play and provide a small snack while we finish our daily tasks. The late Collin Kartchner, an advocate for keeping kids off smartphones, touted the benefits of the eight-second hug. In an interview Kartchner had with mental health counselor Dr. Christy Kane, I learned that eight-second hugs, eight times a day, increase oxytocin levels and happiness levels.[16]

We may not need an overhaul. Small shifts in our daily habits and an awareness of the benefits of in-person living can provide the social stimulus needed for a lifetime of rich friendships and the skills needed to get along well with others.

Discussion Questions

1. Who were some of your favorite friends growing up? Do you still keep in touch with them?
2. In what ways is it harder to form friendships as an adult than as a child? In what ways is it easier?
3. What's one of your favorite things to do with your friends?

Action and Adventure Prompts

1. Invite someone new to do something with you outside.
2. Form a nature group that meets somewhat regularly.
3. Spend time in the playground that nature provides.

seven

The Art of Building a Family

Defining What You Want for Your Days

> To be unaware that a technology comes equipped with a program for social change, to maintain that technology is neutral, to make the assumption that technology is always a friend to culture is, at this hour, stupidity plain and simple.
>
> Neil Postman

I glance around. My bed is unmade, and I'm surrounded by piles. Piles of clothes, piles of books—sorted by "read but need to take notes," "partially read," "haven't read yet but next on my list," "need to read for upcoming podcasts"— and the pile that comes after the "next on my list" pile. There are piles of drawings from my youngest, who's been asking me, "What's your favorite thing to do?" and attempting to capture a picture of her mom (always labeled with the letter "G" so I know for sure) kayaking down a river or reading a book (surprise!). We also have some piles of children's books for bedtime reading and some used dishes stacked up. And, as has always been the case, some toys made their way in here and piled up as well. The one thing I don't have is a cute pile of pillows.

Perusing the scene gives an indication that this is not my ideal life. My insides crave order, and this is anything but. We have five kids we homeschool and a family business, and I'm in the middle of a deadline for a book (this one). Every day is a sorting exercise, where we attempt to deem the order of importance for that twenty-four-hour period, trying to sift the important from the urgent.

Here's what I've determined. These piles are my ideal life, at least for now while our kids are still young, and I don't have the means to make everything perfect. Our choices have led us to this beautiful chaos. We planned for how we wished things would be, and then ultimately there was a reconciliation. A letting go of expectations. A dropping off of many things my soul would delight in (no piles) because today there are kids to hang out with and conversations to have. There are people to encourage and friends to see. There's a path down the road that leads to a yurt, and sometimes we see a woodpecker when we take that walk. The life that I've always dreamed of requires of me a daily surrender, a purposeful laying down of an Instagram-worthy home so we can fit abundance into our daily routine.

We can't do it all. My capacity is much lower than I gave myself credit for pre-kids. But the beautiful thing is that each of us gets to decide what to aim for, what our nonnegotiables are, and what to drop. The key here is knowing that there will be some things you have to drop, so choose wisely.

Ruth Hulburt Hamilton wrote one of my favorite poems, "Song for a Fifth Child." She writes of a house that appears "shocking" because the mother is using her time to blissfully rock her baby instead of clean.[1] That word choice has always struck me. *Shocking.* Some synonyms are "appalling," "awful," "disgusting," "dreadful," and "horrifying"—not any descriptors we want as labels for the homes we inhabit. In fact, a quick trip over to Pinterest reveals that "horrifying" pairs with "monsters" and "disgusting" pairs with "feet." None of these words autofill with "kitchen" or "bedroom." The poem is a reminder that our babies grow, and they grow quickly. There will be time for deep cleaning later.

A few things to note here. The first is that Hamilton wrote this poem for child number five. For many reasons, the majority of families these days don't have that many children. In 2021, there was an average of 1.93 children under the age of eighteen per family in the United States, which is a decrease from 1960, when there was an average of 2.33 kids.[2] But whether you look at the numbers from now or from sixty years ago, we are a far cry from five siblings, so Hamilton's perspective is valuable to us. She didn't learn her lessons until the fifth go-around, and what she tells us is that we must be purposeful to combat the rush to reach milestones and the pressure to keep house. She speaks to the silent cobwebs, "Quiet down." Why? Because they can grow loud in our minds. The dust is ever present, unrelenting, never "sleeping."[3]

Todd Wilson, father of eight, wrote *How to Choose Relationship When There's So Much to Do.* He describes the choice between meaningful time with our kids and the desire to "get stuff done" as a battle.[4]

We all lead complex lives. Through minimalism, through systems and structures, through enlisting outside help, some have found ways to quickly clear the clutter while others are still surrounded by piles of things and some noisy cobwebs. No matter your stance on keeping a home, I've never met a person who has unaccounted-for time spilling out everywhere. Jon Acuff says it this way: "Our time is our most valuable resource, but it is also our most vulnerable."[5] In deciding how we want to craft our family life, we are ultimately making lots of decisions about how to divvy up the time we have control over. The exact amount will vary from family to family and from season to season.

For those of you who are overwhelmed with your surroundings, you may find some answers in chore charts and other places. But I want to clearly convey that when I think back on our kids' early childhood years, I cannot find in my mind's eye any pictures of the actual messes. I know that our house *was* messy, that there were days when toys covered every square inch of the floor. There were seasons of sensory bins where we were always stepping on dry beans. It was annoying, sure, but I cannot conjure up one specific image of any particular day when our home was in shambles.

The images that flood my mind of the early years are pushing a stroller down tree-lined trails, the weight of a baby or toddler on my back. I can picture babies sitting in piles of fall leaves, picking them up, dropping them, and watching them float back down to the top of the pile while sunlight grabbed every twist and turn. My memories flood with boisterous children and their energetic approach to play, having friends over for holiday parties, and the great outdoors.

Determining what you want most for your family may mean you have to drop other things that you also want for your family, but that you want less.

We live in an age of optimization. Traversing back to Pinterest, we find that "the best" leads us to the best chocolate chip cookies, the best chili, the best banana bread, the best party ideas, the best meatloaf, the best ideas for children, and more. But maybe it's all a misnomer. Maybe our lives would be better if we simply made chocolate chip cookies for our friends and our neighbors without concern that they are the best, which is subjective anyway. And how can we even claim to have the best party ideas? I've been to many kinds of parties in my lifetime, all deeply satisfying in their own ways mostly because of the people there and the relationships that were strengthened due to shared experience. The best party ideas almost always include lists and things—napkin holders and butter boards—but none of them hold a candle to our invitees. Pinterest can't help with that part.

A glut of information can cause us to spend lots of time in deep consideration for planning a home—using saved blog posts, magazines, home improvement books, social media, and the friend who has a better eye than we do. We measure twice, cut once. The same type of thought and creativity can go into planning our family heritage. We can look at the totality of what type of family we're hoping to create as an art form with many of the same desired outcomes as interior design—cozy, homey, enticing, and memorable.

I read a lot of information preparing for the birth of our first child, and once he was born, I've hardly had time for reading since. Ironically, parenting thrusts us into an ever-changing world and gives us little or no time to keep up with the transitions. If we aren't purposeful with what we want for our family, the unwanted desires of others may seep in. There are two areas that could use extra consideration: screens and sports.

Can I Refer to You as "Purchasing Friction"?

Without a doubt, you likely view yourself in many ways. You are a parent, a child, a friend, an employee, a cousin, and more. Portions of corporate America give you another role. They see you as an impediment to making money and refer to you as "purchasing friction" since you hold the purse (or wallet) strings for a toy industry that brought in close to three hundred billion dollars in the United States alone in 2021.[6] You're the one who can say no when a child asks for toys, treats, and more. You're the resistance, and your hesitation or refusal to buy stands in the way of higher profits. Eliminating "purchasing friction" is a top goal for many companies. They want to make it easier to "buy now." For those who market their wares to children, loving parents get lumped in with all the other hurdles that slow down the *cha-ching* of the cash register.

Tristan Harris is a technology ethicist. A former Google employee, Harris is the cofounder and executive director of the nonprofit organization Center for Humane Technology, which is concerned with aligning technology and the best interests of humanity. Harris was also the lead role in the documentary *The Social Dilemma*, which brought insight into the behind-the-scenes programming that is subtly persuading us to spend more and more time on social media platforms. Interestingly, Harris was a childhood magician, so his interest in capturing the hearts and minds of humans continued into his adulthood.

A key point from Harris that is echoed in books like *iGen* by Jean Twenge and *Digital Madness* by Nicholas Kardaras is that the insatiable desire social media platforms have for our time and our attention is "destabilizing society."[7] It is affecting our ability to function, let alone thrive.

Facebook launched in 2004, and the iPhone arrived shortly after in 2007. Ten years later, Kardaras's first book, *Glow Kids*, came on the scene. Highly controversial at the time, it sought to prove that our devices were purposefully designed to be addictive. His follow-up book, *Digital Madness*, published in 2022, was the next logical step, as the main tenets in *Glow Kids* are now widely accepted to be true. The main assertions are that the addictive adrenal arousal that happens because of the screens we use is no accident, we can become dependent on stimulation, and "brain development is a fragile process that can easily be disrupted by both understimulation and overstimulation."[8]

As we have a clearer understanding of what a mighty computer in our pockets is doing, Kardaras's second book enlightens us to what is coming (for example, virtual reality headsets for cows to help them produce more milk), how social media is a key contributor to an unhealthy society, and what we can do to "fight for our humanity."[9] His timing is impeccable, as the top five free apps downloaded in 2021 were TikTok, YouTube, Instagram, Snapchat, and Facebook, crowding out apps needed for work productivity, like Gmail and Zoom, and apps like Google Maps that help get us to the places we want to go.[10]

Where the ideas of Harris and Kardaras broadly overlap is in the arena of ethics, which is broadly missing in the conversations about technology. Who is tasked with sounding the alarm about the downsides of new technologies? Is it okay to view parents as "purchasing friction" and attempt to push them out of the company-to-child consumer relationship? No matter the benefits that new technologies provide, there are always associated drawbacks. We must consider if the risks outweigh the rewards.

As we determine the type of family we want to craft, the complexities of electronic distraction are so powerful and invasive that setting them aside for portions of our lives may be one of the only ways we can successfully skirt being a distracted parent and win the battleground in our minds and our homes with Big Tech.

Limiting technology use is beneficial in more ways than one. While handing us our lives back, it also gives us a chance to have in-depth conversations with our kids about "why." *Here's why Netflix has an autoplay feature. Here's why YouTube suggests other videos to watch. Here's why Adam Mosseri, head of Instagram, announces new features such as "Hidden Gems."* Our children need to understand some of what is happening behind the scenes if they are going to have any chance of making informed decisions about technology as they grow and leave our homes. Every "no" and every limit give us opportunities to have age-appropriate conversations about conclusions we've made regarding tech use in our family life.

The art of building a family will include ongoing conversations about the role of technology in your life. Corporations have a clear picture of how they want your family unit to operate, but you are the one who ultimately gets to make the decisions.

Your Kid Probably Isn't Going Pro

Screens aren't the only things that edge their way in and start to take over our lives. Youth sports, extracurriculars, and special tutoring services all appear necessary and are clamoring for a piece of our family pie. Yet contrary to what society is screaming, and even counterintuitive to logical sense, your family needs unfilled time to grow and to form.

Kim John Payne puts it this way in *Simplicity Parenting*: "The pressure is off when childhood is no longer seen as an 'enrichment opportunity' but instead as an unfolding experience—an ecology—with its own pace and natural systems. By consciously backing off the adult sense of 'more!' and 'faster!' and 'earlier!' parents back out of a child's world, protecting it without trying to control it." He also reminds us, "The younger the child, the more free time he or she needs."[11]

In talking with Payne and one of his coauthors and cofounders of Whole Child Sports, Luis Fernando Llosa, parents indicate they are terrified to let their children fall behind in the college athletics competition in particular. They come to Payne and Llosa with pressing questions, wondering if, for instance, age five is far too late to begin one sport or another. In fact, Whole Child Sports was founded for the purpose of raising awareness about the often toxic nature of the youth sports environments and to provide practical advice for families who are struggling through their decisions.

We may think back very fondly on our own childhood days of sports, both club sports and neighborhood pickup games, but the landscape has changed rapidly over the past few decades. Ironically, 70 percent of kids completely give up on sports by age thirteen, before high school even begins, suggesting that for many children and families, the time, money, and effort spent may not be the best allocation of resources. There are even kids who fake injuries as an excuse to sit out.

Researcher, freelance journalist, and former track coach Linda Flanagan wrote a book called *Take Back the Game: How Money and Mania Are Ruining Kids' Sports—and Why It Matters*, in which she exhorts us to consider what adults are getting out of our current sports culture. In a podcast episode we recorded together, she spoke of personally being irrationally delighted or absurdly sad depending on how her son performed in the arena. Parents are often overly invested in these sports outcomes, and Flanagan writes that "no one is honest" about it. As our own lives become more mundane, a shining star athlete seems to add something that is missing, giving us an illusion of wholeness or fulfillment. But Flanagan warns against this. She says that our excessive involvement "signals to kids that grown-ups lead empty and pathetic lives."[12] Ouch.

Her solution? Go cultivate those interests you have! Learn the instrument you've always wanted to play. Call a friend for dinner. Read a thrilling novel. Go for a stroll at the park. Whatever you decide to do, take Flanagan's advice and "flee the bleachers."[13] Not all the time. Show up for some games. Don't miss the championships.

Because we are adults, we innately model to kids what's coming next. If sitting and watching on the sidelines is all that's waiting for them, we aren't giving them much of a reason to grow up. Wouldn't it be great for children to see some adult exuberance? Wouldn't it be exciting for kids to rub shoulders with adults who explore and adventure? Can we give them something to look forward to instead of telling them that right now they are living out the best year they will ever have?

Maybe our jobs are boring, or child-rearing is causing us to hide in the pantry and eat chocolates, but our sole answer cannot be found in the success of our kids. It's too much pressure on them and on us. What life does our child have waiting for them? Let's show them a good one.

There is another group of adults affected by youth sports mania, and it is those who are employed in youth sports, an industry bigger than the entire National Hockey League. Understandably, we all depend on certain things for our livelihood. But knowing that tournaments, travel teams, and specialization can be more in the interest of coaches and businesses than the kids themselves helps us to make informed decisions about involvement level.

Childhood games never used to be the business of adults, and now they are big business. The 700,000-square-foot Disney Wide World of Sports Complex in Orlando, Florida, kicked things off in 1997, and since then 30,000 more sports facilities have opened across the United States, a tenfold increase. There are large budgets and operating costs associated with these buildings, and parents are being sold a dose of fear that is a necessary component to keep these up and running.

Of course, sports can be fun and provide kids with a screen-free environment to move their bodies and make friends, but there is a myth to how far the benefits derived from team sports reach. Flanagan shares, "40 years of research, conducted by more than 20 researchers studying tens of thousands of athletes and nonathletes from youth, high school, collegiate and Olympic levels, simply does not support the notion of sport as a character-building activity, particularly as it applies to sportsmanship behaviors and moral reasoning."[14]

Besides the fact that the benefits may not be what we hope for, there can be harm done to our children through the way we currently pursue organized sports, which includes things like anxiety, depression, sleep deprivation, loneliness, overuse injuries (some of which carry on into adulthood), peer pressure, trouble with coaches, and self-identity issues.

If our child is truly meant to be a superstar, they will find their way. Prodigies "march to the tune of their own drummer," Scott Barry Kaufman tells us in *Ungifted*.[15] It is the child's own instincts and intense interests that are the key ingredients. They manage themselves better than any expert could, which is why we are unable to re-create a Mozart, a Picasso, or a Pascal. We cannot make others be what we want them to become. We cannot force them to excel, and we cannot, no matter how hard we try and how much money we spend, turn them into the best—the starting quarterback, the first-chair violinist, the chess grand master. We can only take a supporting role in the things that drive them and clear out their schedules so they have enough time to indulge.

In *Beyond Winning: Smart Parenting in a Toxic Sports Environment*, Kim John Payne, Luis Fernando Llosa, and Scott Lancaster inform us, "The best athletes in the world have had formal training at some stage, but what distinguishes them from the rest is what they did as kids when they were alone or with friends, just messing around."[16]

It isn't an air of professionalism that gives kids a leg up for future success; it's the opposite. It's play. It's spontaneity. In *Miseducation: Preschoolers at Risk*, author Dr. David Elkind gives us the formula for success. It is "not the product of acquired academic skills; rather, success in life is the product of a healthy personality."[17]

As far as sports, screens, and all extracurricular activities go, knowing all who benefit and why when it comes to shelling out our family time can help us maintain balance. Who is profiting most from our decisions? Is it us, or is it a corporation? Are we living the life we really want to lead? Does it truly make sense to view childhood as a mad dash to some arbitrary finish line? Is earlier better? Or can we pump the brakes, knowing full well that the unhampered play of children gives advantages for today as well as tomorrow?

Don't Worry, Be Happy

If you could parent from a place knowing full well that your child will "turn out," how might you approach today differently? If you were able to scrub all the fear and uncertainty out of what's driving your decision-making by getting a quick glimpse into a stable, secure, and happy future, how might you structure your days?

You haven't prepared a meal? You haven't shopped? The kids are squabbling in the yard? Modern parenting says you're done. You're in for it. And yet Ruth Hulburt Hamilton was onto something. Kids grow up. There is nothing we can do to stop it. And maybe all our fear, all our stuffing and enhancing and coercing, isn't accomplishing what we are hoping it will. Can we be present with the lives before us and trust their individual paths to appear before them, one step at a time?

What is the vision you want to pass on? What are the truths you want to live out? What experiences do you want to have? What games do you want to play, books do you want to read, pies do you want to bake? We've been duped into thinking it's our standardized test scores and our rankings that determine our tomorrow, when really it's how fully we live today.

Dr. Madeline Levine remarks in *Ready or Not: Preparing Our Kids to Thrive in an Uncertain and Rapidly Changing World* that the "metrics we've always used" to measure childhood success are becoming obsolete anyway. They are no longer trustworthy assessments. "Adaptability is the sustaining feature of those who not only survive but who thrive," she says.[18] I don't adapt when I'm given detailed, step-by-step instructions. I adapt when things are uncertain, when the ball curves and I wasn't expecting it. Marriage has caused me to adapt, as has childbirth, job loss, and more. What Levine says makes sense: "If our children are to thrive in a world that is rapidly evolving and full of uncertainty, they need less structure and more play."[19]

Shout it from the rooftops! Here is the hope! We can shed the rigid assessments of what others say childhood should be for whatever we want our family life to be. The rules have changed, and now we can dream.

My own life is unrecognizable to me. Three years of abysmal failure in early motherhood somehow landed me here, a mathematician writing the nonfiction book in your hands. I don't think we can fully prepare for our future life. We can, with some certainty, predict tomorrow and possibly a few days from now, even a week. But what about a month from now, let alone a year or a handful of them? Levine writes, "The vast majority of adults who consider themselves successful have had winding (what I call 'squiggly') life paths."[20]

In a rapidly changing world, we are preparing our kids for the squiggle. And since we don't know what that squiggle will look like, our best bet is to live life with gusto. To make it what we want instead of having it dictated to us by those who will profit off our fear.

The world is out there. It's ready for us to make of our family what we will. To create a family rhythm that is inviting, invigorating, and unique to the individuals and brings out the best in each family member. Intentionality, an understanding of the forces that influence our decisions, and deep regard for the value of play help us know what we truly want for our family. Taking the time to decide what we want for our days, determining how we spend our time when the choice is ours, can serve as a guide as we navigate the pressures of our world.

Grow Old Along with Me

In *The Wild + Free Family*, Ainsley Arment writes about how family culture leaks. We can derive a twofold meaning here. How we structure our family influences others. What an honor to know that our sincere choices will leak out into the greater culture and affect what others do. But also, as the culture we have chosen leaks out as if through small spaces in a colander, we have to be on guard that we don't lose it completely.

This was an aha moment for me. I understood why so often we're spurred on to start something new, a tradition or a new habit that we're motivated to include into our family rhythm, but we're never able to hold on to it for all that long. It's because there are holes in our intentions, driven in by all sorts of societal distractions and even our own ineptitudes, and out our traditions go through the holes, drip by drip. We must build a lifestyle in which we consistently mend the holes because they are going to keep coming, one by one. An invitation here. A sparkling new opportunity there. Plus, car repairs, dirty dishes, diaper changes, illness, weary nights, allergies, and all manner of things that put hurdles in our everyday.

We must choose how we want to design our family, how we will grow old together. This is an imperative because for those who don't choose that design, "one will be assigned to you by society at large," according to Arment.[21] Once you have drawn your line in the sand, you are then signed up to be "relentless defenders" of the culture you have created so that it doesn't all leak out, leaving space for the whims of the tech gods, the CEOs of the sports facilities, and the administrators who are trying to increase test scores to determine the overall direction for your family.

There are other undercurrents as well. American computer scientist, author, inventor, and futurist Ray Kurzweil has been making projections about the future of technology since the 1980s, to the tune of 86 percent accuracy.[22] He continues to do so, writing in his 2005 book *The Singularity Is Near*, "Within several decades information-based technologies will encompass all human knowledge and proficiency, ultimately including the pattern-recognition powers, problem-solving skills, and emotional and moral intelligence of the human brain itself." He mentions the limits of our humanity, our brains that are "several million times slower than contemporary electronic circuits" and the "cumbersome maintenance rituals" that our "version 1.0 biological bodies" require.[23] And I feel these limitations. Interestingly, we've begun to use machinist language when referring to our bodies with statements like "taking time to recharge."

Kurzweil refers to "the Singularity" as the "culmination of the merger of our biological thinking and existence with our technology, resulting in a world that is still human but that transcends our biological roots. There will be no distinction, post-Singularity, between human and machine or between physical and virtual reality."[24] A sequel to his book releases in 2024 with the chilling title *The Singularity Is Nearer*.

Of course, some will correctly say that certain advancements in technology are enhancing and even saving lives, but as Dr. Kardaras teaches in *Digital Madness*, "Wonderful innovations always have come at a price."[25] There is great promise, but it comes with risk. There are unknown hazards, things we could never predict, so we are always backpedaling. But what happens when we can't get those pedals going backward fast enough?

All of this is rather disconcerting. Suddenly, the old saying "Grow old along with me; the best is yet to be" looks a little bleaker. "Grow old along with me; sooner or later we might turn into computers."

Yet here is what I believe: within the four walls of our homes and collectively as we make decisions as families, we still hold the power to pull back, to limit, to guard, to simplify. We can move the needle. Maybe I'm naive, but what I see is that small changes toward connecting more and living hands-on make a considerable impact. We realize we don't need so much of what the digital overlords are offering us.

Kurzweil even predicts a changing nature of play. "By the 2020s, full-immersion virtual reality will be a vast playground of compelling environments and experiences. Although the environments will not be completely convincing at first, by the late 2020s they will be indistinguishable from real reality and will involve all of the senses, as well as neurological correlations of our emotions."[26] What a twist on the word "playground," which has historically been referred to as an outdoor play space for kids.

Mark Zuckerberg is well on his way to walking us down a path toward a digital dreamworld where societal sedation is the norm. He's even giving away the virtual reality glasses we will need for his "metaverse." How generous! Taking it just one decade further, "As we enter the 2030s there won't be clear distinctions between human and machine, between real and virtual reality, or between work and play."[27]

We've been warned, and this is dire. Backpedaling from content that streams 24/7 is one thing. This is a different animal entirely.

Founded in 2016, Elon Musk's Neuralink Corporation is currently undergoing human trials. Citing that the original intention is for medical assistance, Neuralink is "aiming to design a fully implantable, cosmetically invisible brain-computer interface to let you control a computer or mobile device anywhere you go."[28]

The time has come to have convictions about how we are going to build our families and how we are going to raise our children, considering the technologies that are exploding around us. Kardaras warns again, "Humanity's most ambitious inventions and technological advances are inseparable from their dark side."[29] If we don't make the changes now, maybe there will come a time when we no longer have the chance to define our days. Our kids have to know, in age-appropriate ways, some of what is going on so that when the time comes for them, they will also have the chance to infuse their own styles into family building.

One of the most eye-opening books I've ever read was written when I was five years old. It was the year of Microsoft 1.0, the first *Back to the Future* movie, and the year Tommy Hilfiger came out with a men's line. That year, Neil Postman wrote a book about the fundamental societal changes caused by television called *Amusing Ourselves to Death*, a title that could aptly apply today. In the book, he parallels concepts from *Brave New World* by Aldous Huxley with concepts from *1984* by George Orwell. We're on the lookout for the Big Brother that Orwell spoke of, but Huxley painted a picture of a different world, one in which "people will come to love their oppression, to adore the technologies that undo their capacities to think."[30]

In a riveting way, Postman walks us through the disorientation that comes through information overload, broken attention, and living globally. But he doesn't leave us without hope. The answer he gives involves knowledge. "No medium is excessively dangerous if its users understand what its dangers are. To ask is to break the spell."[31] This is an interesting choice of words, as Ray Kurzweil was an avid magician as a child. "I replaced my parlor magic with technology projects," he writes.[32] As you will recall, Tristan Harris, who "explored the influences that hijack human attitudes, behaviors, and beliefs,"[33] was also a childhood magician. Bill Gates, who supports what are known as "Magic Seeds"[34] to combat world hunger, would say that Steve Jobs "cast spells"[35] on his audiences during presentations.

Now is the time to reflect on the kind of life we want to live and the kind of life we want to hand our children. It's the time to question, to learn, to defy, to banter, to entertain ourselves, to pull others along with us. These things have become nonnegotiables as we strive to build our families and remember who we are.

Discussion Questions

1. What was your family life like growing up? What are some things you took from your family of origin into your current life? What are some things you changed?
2. How much thought have you given to the type of family life you want to create?
3. How do you handle not being able to "do it all" when it comes to everything adults have to juggle? Do you struggle with perfectionism, or are you able to let things go?

Action and Adventure Prompts

1. Write a family mission statement.
2. Gather a group of kids and cheer them on as they play a pickup game of sports. Watch firsthand all the negotiation and compromise that is happening.
3. Do something that models an exuberant adult life to your kids.

eight

I Don't Remember the Quadratic Formula

Create Learning That Lasts

The primary goal of real education is not to deliver facts but to guide students to the truths that will allow them to take responsibility for their lives.

John Taylor Gatto

It was the back of the bag of store-bought bread, in comparison to the ingredients list I had in front of me, that spurred me on to make homemade bread, and about ten years ago, I made my first loaf from scratch. Flour, sugar, salt, yeast, water or milk, and oil or butter can be transformed into something that provides so much. The rising dough brings all the kids together. Given the sophistication of modern-day toys, it's surprising how engaging a lump of dough and a teaspoon of flour can be. The smell of bread baking brings the family together from all parts of the house, and there's nothing quite like a slice of warm, homemade bread. It goes with just about every meal and is the perfect complement to your read-aloud time and nearly anything else. Who doesn't love homemade bread?

Baking bread is one of the only things I've learned on my first try. My typical route is to fail miserably, adjust, and then succeed, but bread seems fairly foolproof. The only detail I've found to be tricky is the temperature of the liquid. Whether you're using milk or water, the temperature has to be within a certain range—warm enough so that you activate the yeast but not so warm that you kill it. A small kitchen thermometer does wonders, but you can clearly see if the yeast froths or not, signaling that it has been activated and will go to work.

Over the years, I've really only messed up the bread twice. Once I burned the yeast, and therefore it didn't activate and the dough didn't rise. The other time I forgot the salt, which inhibits the dough from rising too fast, so sadly, that loaf didn't turn out either. These two mistakes come to mind each time I embark on baking a new loaf, yet I haven't made them again. Bread baking has since expanded to dinner rolls, bagels, pretzels, pizza dough, breadsticks, and more because the process (and even the ingredient list) is basically the same.

Learning as an adult has a very different look and feel than school learning did, and the outcomes seem different as well. In the all-too-common case of pulling out of the oven a dozen homemade bagels that our kids promptly devour, I have both acquired and used a tangible skill. Baking bread was a self-initiated pursuit that led to something that is truly worthwhile in our family, and also one that I thoroughly enjoy. It was rather easy to learn, and the few setbacks I encountered became my future teachers, because who has time or ingredients to waste when everyone is anticipating a piping hot, fresh loaf of bread? Mistakes are excellent teachers, and we really need to increase our tolerance for failing.

I wonder what else exists that I'm unaware of that would provide similar joy and excitement. I think about those for whom homemade dough isn't quite as interesting, yet they've found other things that compel them to learn. Of the millions of things there are to explore, how did we end up with such a narrow focus? Of course, practicality is a valid point at times. As a child, I would have comprehended fractions much easier by doubling or tripling a bread recipe, but my math classroom didn't have an attached kitchen.

I know we've made some strides in project-based learning approaches, but that isn't the point. Project-based learning still mainly runs on the questions and parameters someone else has set forth. We can learn a great deal about the world, in a somewhat unsystematic approach, through a deep dive into our own interests. If the current school environments aren't able to logistically provide those opportunities at scale, then out-of-school hours should, at least partially. Yet large amounts of schoolwork continue to follow kids home.

We have only so many hours. Childhood lasts for only a finite period. Adult responsibilities often preclude us from that deep dive into the grandness of life where we can tinker and experiment, trying on different topics for size in order to discover our inner drives. When we fiercely protect the open spaces of childhood, not giving too much of them away to virtual experiences or even well-intentioned homework assignments, we give our kids advantages that cannot be measured. Who's to say where our paths would lead if we're given the opportunity to start finding ourselves during the childhood years? Where might we be? What might we be doing?

It's as if childhood these days is filled with a fog. Kids cannot see clearly because they are inundated with the expectations of those they will never meet. Rich Karlgaard, author of *Late Bloomers*, says, "Kids often have little time or room for self-exploration. They are shuttled onto the conveyor belt, moving in one direction, with no encouragement of other interests or career choices. The conveyor belt moves them along a narrow path of success and starves them of opportunities for self-discovery."[1]

When we talk of learning that sticks, there are two types of learning that appear most valuable for our current and future selves, but these are rarely found in a traditional setting. The first type is learning about what drives us, and the second is learning how to learn. "What's your favorite subject?" is thrown around so often, but the answer choices are sorely limited. This question has become something of a multiple-choice test question with four answer options: (A) Math, (B) English, (C) Science, (D) History.

But so many subject areas weave in and out of each other. For example, did you know that both grizzly bears and black bears can eat up to forty thousand moths a day and that scientists have determined this by analyzing bear scat? Studying this one interesting phenomenon could include learning about geography (where do these types of bears live?), number sense (how big is forty thousand?), science (what else is interesting about bears?), and career paths (I could study animal poop for a living?).

And speaking of scat, did you know there is only one animal that has cube-shaped poop? The Australian, bare-nosed wombat excretes around one hundred six-sided droppings a day. Then they stack their poop cubes together to mark their territory. I remember holding plastic and wooden 3D models of shapes in geometry class, but exposure to a replica of a wombat poop cube would've given the information needed *and* opened the door to so many more exploratory questions. Why is it a cube? Does that have to do with the wombat's intestines? Where do wombats live? What do they look like? What do they eat? What are the people who study these animals called? Are there any other animals that have unique scat shapes?

1000 Hours Outside has an accompanying nature curriculum called "Add the Wonder Nature Curriculum," through which families learn all about our planet within the context of fascinating things in our world, like bear scat and wombat scat.

When we follow the path of curiosity, it leads to discovery and even accidental learning. It reminds me of the volunteer flowers and plants that sometimes pop up in the garden. Somehow the seeds were scattered, and we got more than we bargained for. This is what happens with curiosity-led learning. Tangents arise, and we learn more than we ever anticipated.

Go to new places. Meet more people. Make lots of choices along the way. Do challenging things and consider what can be learned through simple means like making a pot of soup. What grips one child may not interest another, but thankfully our world offers unlimited channels through which we can learn in-depth information about any subject through unconventional means.

In *The Call of the Wild + Free*, Ainsley Arment writes, "Children need better public relations."[2] It's true. We deem ourselves the chauffeurs, but kids can take us so many places with their interests and desires, opening our eyes to a bigger world if we allow them to. Children are energetic, playful, boisterous, passionate, intense, hopeful, vivacious, spontaneous, enthusiastic, curious, intelligent, expressive, generous, and forgiving. In many ways, we should strive for what they have and fiercely resist the slow drain of these qualities that often happens throughout the childhood years. Instead of fighting for test scores, let's fight to value what children already possess. Book learning is unnatural. It is the experiment. Kids join us with tremendous characteristics, and we carelessly let them slip away. One of my biggest surprises as a parent is how much I have learned through the interests and exuberance of our kids. The world offers us an endless array of fascinating things to learn about, and children remind us of that. Let them guide us.

An easy practice to add to your nature habit is to keep a calendar of firsts. The first snowfall, the first apple blossoms, the first tadpoles, the first wildflowers, the first mosquito bite, the first camping trip. These small observations help us see connections and rhythms that exist around us. They remind us to truly see and to notice all the wonder that is constantly popping up, season after season, year after year.

In a rapidly changing world, it's helpful to have a pool of interests to draw from as things like job markets ebb and flow. These things emerge only when there is time for play and exploration. Time must be carved out. Our lives are often indescribably full, and the opportunities keep flowing in. There are solid justifications for everything we choose to stuff in, but is it all truly necessary? Carving out involves a deliberate removal, the winnowing away of parts of the whole to create something unique and beautiful. This is what we must do for our lives, for our children, because learning about ourselves is a foundational piece to lifelong fulfillment.

What are you learning about right now? Maybe lots, maybe not much. But in order to learn anything, you must allot time to it. Whether you're reading a book, having a discussion, or trying your hand at something new, growth and knowledge come only when you give significant space to the process of learning.

This space also gives us the opportunities to see our children and our students in a new light. It invites us to come aboard their train and encourage them in the direction they are headed. Children are not cogs in a machine, though someone looking at how we currently structure childhood might come to that conclusion. Children are uniquely wonderful individuals with many facets that need exploring, and they need mentors who encourage them through their unique steps ahead. Education should prize individuality because robots have already taken over the assembly lines.

What the world needs is our distinctiveness and the wonderful, even peculiar hobbies and interests that we can hardly find the time for. We need to cease the "These are the best years of your life" commentaries. Growing up is exciting. Let's showcase for our kids that there's something to look forward to. In *Play It Away: A Workaholic's Cure for Anxiety*, Charlie Hoehn went back to his childhood roots and started playing home-run derby with a friend once a week. How fun is that! We don't have to—and we shouldn't—stop playing just because we've finished school or hit some arbitrary age marker.

The world ahead is going to need a generation of kids who are celebrated for their unrepeatability and who are bold enough to thrive in the midst of mediocrity. Now is when we unleash time and allow our kids to try on a variety of fascinations for size. Bring back the dabbling, the tinkering, the exploration. Allow children to emerge from their formative years with an immense knowledge base of themselves. This type of learning will go hand in hand with them throughout their lifetimes.

Beyond learning about themselves, childhood is a time when kids learn how to learn. This may not be necessary for all, as kids enter the world with all the processes in place to innately master vast feats of knowledge and movement. But a large swath of children loses this innate sense over the course of many years of adult direction. The lesson plans for a two-year-old to learn a new language look nothing like the lesson plans for a middle-school classroom ready to embark on learning a new tongue. The two-year-old has no lesson plans and yet learns through immersion, practice, and delight. Slight corrections are often all that are needed to grasp the subtle differences of tenses and pluralities. What a miracle!

Early childhood is filled with autodidacts, those who are self-taught. So where do they go? American author and educator John Holt wrote a short book called *Learning All the Time: How Small Children Begin to Read, Write, Count, and Investigate the World, without Being Taught*. The subtitle might make many of us scratch our heads. There's no way. How can young children possibly learn these things without a teacher? We've lost the collective knowledge that we are born with the capacity to self-teach. It is not the lessons of others that cause us to lose that ability throughout the childhood years. It is not the well-designed, adult-derived lesson plans that detract from a child's innate capacity to learn new skills at a level of mastery. It's all the time we have taken away that has caused them to forget what they are capable of.

There are arguments pro-screen and many that are anti-screen, and there are some circumstances where screens are an absolute necessity. Outside of those circumstances, however, it is the combination of screens, schoolwork, homework, and enrollment in adult-directed extracurriculars that is gobbling up every bit of time children need to continue on in their self-learning. Often they lose the skill set entirely.

This skill set includes not only the incremental learning steps that come from feedback in the environment but also the joy that comes when all of our practice and striving finally click. We've done it! We learn that learning is exciting. That it is intrinsically rewarding. That we are able to hold our own attention for the length of time required for mastery. That we are capable of more than we think. And that there is always more wonderful learning to look forward to. We never fully exhaust that which may be known.

If only we could take the fearlessness and the resolve of a thirteen-month-old learning both to walk and to talk into the rest of our lives. Many prominent authors attribute their success to being self-taught. American novelist and short-story writer Ernest Hemingway was a voracious reader. His sister, Marcelline, spoke of how he read anything he could get his hands on in their home and that he read "for hours at a time in bed."[3] American author and screenwriter Ray Bradbury is quoted as saying, "Libraries raised me,"[4] which could be interpreted as Bradbury raising himself. The library is simply a tool, and he chose how to use this tool at his fingertips.

Beyond authors, there are scores of musicians, artists, architects, engineers, scientists, historians, entrepreneurs, and educators who echo the often-sung refrains of autodidacts. Henry David Thoreau said, "How could youths better learn to live than by at once trying the experiment of living?"[5] This is the charge of the self-learner. Go live. And through living, learn.

Within the structures and confines of current society, what are the chances of maintaining or reviving the capacity for self-instruction? They are high if we take our foot off the gas pedal, if we slide the screens out of sight, and if we trust that what a child perceives as a worthy endeavor is indeed a worthy endeavor.

I Do Remember the Quadratic Formula

I titled this chapter "I Don't Remember the Quadratic Formula," but I must confess, I actually do. Beyond that, I can recall what to use it for, though you may be surprised to know that I never actually have outside of a school setting. I taught the formula for years as a high school math teacher, and it hasn't exited my mind yet. But I've begun to notice that many other things have, when my friends' kids who are hitting the high school years come to me with questions.

I've embodied the "teaching someone else is the best way to learn" approach, but to what end? Where does our memorization take us? In my case, it took me to another four years of my life given to a college degree and a good deal of money spent doing so, then on to a short stint of a career, and now to a place where I use my acquired knowledge only for brief and somewhat shaky texts with a few teenagers. I say this not out of a place of cynicism but out of deep thought, knowing mine is not the only experience like this. We trade our lives for a certain type of learning that is void of experience, and maybe we are better off for it, but it's equally likely that we are not.

In a series called *Book TV: Television for Serious Readers*— a title that strikes me as odd—American author and thirty-year schoolteacher John Taylor Gatto said, "Nobody can educate you except yourself. You can be trained from outside but only educated from within. One is a matter of habit and memory and the other is the matter of learning how to seize the initiative."[6]

When I write and speak about spending time outdoors— the real versus the virtual—it is not for the sake of vilifying the screen but instead for an awareness of the importance of balance. The same intention lies here, at the heart of learning. This consideration is important, as school-type learning takes up the vast majority of childhood hours for most kids. But this is primarily the "habit and memory" part Gatto speaks of, where kids are "trained from outside." I think that because this distinction has not been made clear, we've lost sight of a balanced approach to education, one that includes large amounts of firsthand experiences that cannot be easily and readily doled out in a traditional class-room setting.

In his book *The Harm of Coercive Schooling*, Dr. Peter Gray writes of a young man named Sam who struggled with school, graduating from high school at the bottom of his class, but then went on in his twenties to become a very successful chef. Gray makes some bold statements about this story, such as Sam "learned nothing from his 13 years of public schooling." After a rough school career, "the good part of his life began."[7] What a reminder that if your child is struggling through school, all is not lost. The drudgeries of childhood aren't always (ever?) necessary precursors to a satisfying life.

Because traditional learning has grown in the time it requires (for example, homework for the early elementary grades), we are left with ever smaller portions of hours and minutes at our disposal for our kids to learn how to "seize the initiative." But unlike so many other problems we encounter in life, the answer to this one is easier done than said. It hinges on awareness of and trust in the riches of childhood wanderings.

When we first started spending large parts of our days under the open sky, I was simply unaware of the vast benefits to mind, body, and soul that accompanied those excursions. There is, I believe, a collective unawareness, as evidenced by the lack of children in the forests. Additionally, we're inundated with so many worthy programs that depend financially on this unawareness. Our children already possess the innate capacity to be an independent producer, a creator, and a worthwhile director of empty time. We've just forgotten that. Maybe it doesn't seem like this as the child throws their cup repeatedly off their high chair or asks to read the same Eric Carle book again and again or flails their body with complaints of boredom, but these young souls have something in them that you and I do not.

The thrown cup teaches a young child much about the world. If you were stuck in a chair, what might you do? Possibly throw the cup as well? The child is learning not only about physics but also about responses and reactions and, with age, a bit about societal expectations, manners, and self-control. The well-worn board book is just another step on the path of mastery learning. A bored child becomes adept at finding opportunities.

So, what must we do? In a word: less. We must hang the van keys on their hook and leave them there several afternoons of the week. We have to de-emphasize the homework that seeks to extend an already lengthy school day. In *The Discovery of a Child*, Maria Montessori exhorts us "to cast a ray of light and pass on." She elaborates with, "To stimulate life, leaving it free, however, to unfold itself, that is the first duty of the educator."[8]

For so long we've seen education and thought "more." How much more can we fit in? How much earlier can we start? Change comes from seeing education in a different light, or at least realizing that the individualized component of learning does not readily occur at scale within a system that depends on conformity to function.

In talking about learning that sticks, we are encompassing many delineations. It's about the things we know, the things we know how to do, the processes by which we learn and grow, and the pieces we've picked up about ourselves along the way. It's also about life lessons. These accompany any childhood that is filled with hands-on experiences. Kids who play, and especially kids who play outdoors, are learning to have increased tolerance toward uncomfortable situations. They are learning how to deal with impermanence, when close friends move away or even when play is done for the evening. They are learning how to make quick decisions, how to adjust to circumstances that are beyond their control. They are learning patience and resourcefulness and how to deal with annoyances. They are learning that it's within their power to find things in this world that make them thrive.

My husband and I had a discussion the other afternoon with our teenagers while we hiked. They said if you're on a treadmill, you can just step off whenever you want, but when you've embarked on a trail, you're committed until you reach the end. There's no easy out, but there is usually a feeling of accomplishment at the end. Metaphors for life abound in nature, and childhood experiences lay a foundation for the trials that will come later in life.

In August 2021, I started interviewing people for my podcast, which was an extensive exercise in my own learning. I end each podcast with the same question: "What is a favorite outdoor memory of yours from childhood?" The answers have been nothing less than simplistic beauty, a reminder that we can find what we are looking for in our everyday and that our children are not seeking the grandiose. They are supremely satisfied with memories like the following:

It was those days of "Be home before dark," and so we would rally up a couple neighbor kids that were all different ages. And we would go exploring in the canyon and put snacks in a backpack and be gone all day. And those memories of that freedom and that time spent outside were really formative for me.

Mary Heffernan, rancher at Five Marys Farms

When I was in fourth grade, Halley's Comet came around, and my fourth-grade teacher organized a 4 a.m. field trip. I'm going to cry even talking about it. My mom volunteered to drive a group up there. It was maybe the first time I had been out in the stars. We watched it in a mountainous area, and it was just about the novelty of being up so early. It was so special, the fact that my mom who was a full-time single mom could never really volunteer, but she could go at 4 a.m.

Katy Bowman, founder of Nutritious Movement

I was probably eleven years old, and sometimes I would get up early in the morning and go fishing before school. When I did this I was by myself. I couldn't get any of my friends to get up that early. So I'd bicycle down to this river and fish. And this particular memory that I had, it was spring in northern Minnesota, the snow was melting so there was still some snow on the side, but it was a sunny morning. And I just remember being there and maybe for the first time seeing how beautiful the world is.

Dr. Peter Gray, author of *Free to Learn*

Going on my bike in Lima over to a general park and watching tadpoles in the pond and then going back a few days later and seeing that they'd grown into a different stage. And just riding around on my bike with my dog and looking for somebody to play with, not knowing if I was going to find somebody to play with and therefore making new friends in weird places all over. There was a freedom to it all.

Luis Fernando Llosa, coauthor of *Emotionally Resilient Teens and Tweens*

Sometimes you don't realize how significant these childhood memories are until way later in life. When I was around six, seven, or eight, my grandfather had a large garden, and he surrounded that garden with a trellis of concord grapes. By the time we could visit my grandparents in the summer, it was always when the grapes were ripe. As a little child, I would walk out under those grape arbors and they seemed to stretch forever, but they were probably only 100 feet by 100 feet. I was just barely tall enough to reach the bottom ones hanging down, and, of course, there were all those yellow bees in there buzzing, but what I remember is being able to walk out there and be nestled in abundance. It was like a womb embrace of abundance. That has framed my vision and dream. I want to step out the back door every morning and be immersed in this womb of abundance that a benevolent Creator has bestowed upon me. He has even given me the privilege of being his hands and feet to massage it, caress it, and nurture it in his place as a surrogate caretaker, and that is a profound responsibility and opportunity.

Joel Salatin, co-owner of Polyface Farm

Take a moment to think of a favorite outdoor memory from your childhood. After Dr. Peter Gray talked about his early morning solo fishing trips, he spoke about how many of the large, transformational moments that happen during our childhoods are often away from adult supervision. The presence of a grown-up changes the environment, yet there are kids today who speak of being under watchful eyes—surveillance, if you will—constantly.

It's Never Too Late

It's easy to believe we've run out of the time needed to make a difference, but creativity starts flowing almost immediately when we have nothing to do. Boredom is a state our brains and bodies want to flee from, so when we remove stimulation, we've created fertile soil for imagination. We can begin today by carving out a small window of time that allows for self-direction and then see where it goes.

Luis Fernando Llosa writes in *Beyond Winning*, "Consider your hesitation a blessing, and hold onto it for dear life. What your instincts are telling you is that your child's childhood really matters. Protecting and extending it for as long as possible is one of our biggest responsibilities as parents."[9]

One of my favorite conversations on my podcast was with John Muir Laws (who goes by Jack), artist, naturalist, author, and educator. The topic was nature journaling, and at the time I didn't do that, so I felt some trepidation about the conversation. A nature journal is a place to write or draw about things seen or experienced in the natural world. I wondered how we would fill an hour's worth of time on this one simple concept. To date, this episode is the longest on the podcast because we ended up talking for almost two hours, during which time I cried and Jack played the ukulele. He messed up many times, displaying that almost all of us will be bad at something when we first begin.

Our discussion went far beyond nature journaling and centered on a growth mindset. Can we grow? Can we get better? Can we overcome our fears?

Jack said that there are two areas in life where a fixed mindset about our abilities often takes hold—math and art. These are the subjects that cause many people to say, "I can't" and "I won't ever be able to." One reason to nature journal is to acquire a growth mindset. Jack assures us that in looking back over even six weeks of drawings in our journals, we will see progress.

Jon Acuff tells us, "Gather evidence that reminds you how capable you really are,"[10] and it's solid advice. The future is uncertain, and we need to have things we can point to that propel us forward with confidence in our capabilities. Our kids are going to take their cues from us. Are we growing? Are we diving into something new, knowing full well we won't be good at it yet? Are we stretching ourselves?

It's helpful to know that though it has become exacerbated, our struggle with balancing our time is not a new phenomenon. Baroness Maria Augusta Trapp, singer and stepmother of the Trapp Family Singers, wrote this in her 1949 memoir: "Our age has become so mechanical that this has also affected our recreation. People have gotten used to sitting down and watching a movie, a ball game, a television set. It may be good once in a while, but it certainly isn't good all the time. Our own faculties, our imagination, our memory, the ability to do things with our mind and our hands—they need to be exercised. If we become too passive, we get dissatisfied."[11]

It's that last sentence that may explain so much of what is going on with our children and the rising internal struggles they are facing. In a well-intentioned pursuit of their success, we have taken the reins of their lives and left them as passive participants. An unlimited rise in the availability of screen consumption has done the same thing. Whereas in generations past, the boundaries existed within the constructs of society, today the opportunities for passive entertainment are infinite. Between video games, social media, video streaming, and innumerable television networks, entertainment is always available, and for those with smartphones, it's right there in a pocket or potentially in a hand already. We are not meant to live the majority of our lives in a passive way. We are innovators and imaginers. We can create worlds within our worlds. We are dreamers and doers.

If concerns about your child's academic success are keeping you up at night, celebrate that times have changed. There isn't one straight line to a life of fulfillment anymore. Think about the nontraditional subjects they are interested in, and remember that all learning counts, all growth counts. Interest and intrinsic motivation help what is learned to be remembered for the long haul. What great news! Live fully today. That's what will prepare you for tomorrow.

Discussion Questions

1. What are some things you remember from your school years?
2. What were some of your favorite things to learn about when you were growing up? Did you learn them in the school environment or outside of it?
3. What's something new that you're learning about today? Is there something you've been wanting to try but haven't yet?

Action and Adventure Prompts

1. Teach someone else something you know.
2. Learn a new skill. Involve your family if it's a good fit for everyone.
3. Be brave and do something that you aren't completely comfortable with and that makes you a little scared.

nine

The Dynamic Duo

The Transformative Power of Free Play in Nature

Play is not recess from education; it IS education. Children learn far more in play, and with far more joy, than they could possibly learn in a classroom.

Dr. Peter Gray, *Mother Nature's Pedagogy*

When the broader society included more margin, our lives had more margin too. As I mentioned in chapter 4, there used to be space naturally built into childhood. Our vehicles didn't have screens, our phones didn't have Wi-Fi, our televisions had less programming, our sports programs weren't so all-encompassing, our schools gave less homework. We had expanded opportunities to utilize our inner motivations and find things to do that gave us satisfaction.

Today and for the foreseeable future, we have to build in those margins; we have to fight for them. We have to pay close attention to where our time is fleeing, and there often doesn't seem to be enough of it. I think back to my own childhood, of open-ended afternoons and weekends. Time seemed more freely available then.

With our hours and minutes more accounted for these days, there is a natural desire to make the most of what we have. Combining time for free play and time in nature does just that. It is a power duo that bestows endless joy but also lifelong developmental benefits. Even just taking your everyday indoor activities out under the blue sky will enhance your life. Can you fold your laundry outside? Drink your coffee? Play a board game? Do your schoolwork? Read a book? Prep a meal? Nature makes us feel better no matter what we're doing outside.

Add in the component of free play, which might be better worded as subtracting the adult-directed instructions, and you'll be looking at long-term benefits to cognition, social skills, physical health, and emotional health. I've discussed many of these gains throughout the book, but in this chapter the focus is on unstructured time in nature. When free play and nature combine forces, the stars align.

Take a simple balance beam, for instance. I had one in my gym class growing up. I don't remember the exact particulars of length and width, but I do know that it never changed. That balance beam was the one that was always used, maybe even to this very day. No matter where it happens, working on the skill of balance is excellent for both physical and cognitive health. It's a skill we should continue to prize long after our school days are over.

It's clear to see how nature amplifies the experience of working on balance. Starting at young ages, long before elementary-school gym days, kids seek out balancing opportunities—and nature provides them abundantly. Our own kids would walk on curbs and on the curb stops in parking lots. They would climb up on stumps or fallen tree trunks, testing their balancing abilities as they stood in one spot on a wobbly surface or attempted to walk from one end to the other, occasionally suspended over a small stream. The variability of these types of situations is immeasurable. Balancing on a balance beam and on a knotty, uneven tree trunk are in many ways the same, but they are also very different. The indoors is static; the outdoors is dynamic. If we can take a child outside, at least on occasion, and let them roam in a safe environment, then they can seek out the developmental input that their bodies need because nature offers an abundance of opportunities.

As parents, we don't want one more thing to do. I get it. It's all too much to begin with. In my early years of mothering, if I had been told I needed to do all I was doing now *and* tack on three hours of outdoor play most days, I would've been crushed by the enormity of the ask. But this is not about more; this is different. This is a shift. It's a way of doing life that allows for a slower pace, a fulfilling life, and all the benefits we are hoping to bestow during childhood—and more that we weren't even aware of.

Movement Is Learning

I don't know about you, but when I think of learning, even after all the research I've done, my mind still jumps to the classroom setting. It jumps to pencils and chalkboards and workbooks and studying and research. If we could expand our view of learning to confidently include moments of childhood elation, our world would change. American educator John Holt says it this way: "Living is learning and when kids are living fully and energetically and happily they are learning a lot, even if we don't always know what it is."[1]

The energetic movement woven into our K-12 schooling paradigm includes gym class and recess, time shuffling between classes or through the lunch line, and getting up to sharpen a pencil. In certain cases, teachers have implemented movement breaks throughout the day—a set of jumping jacks, let's say—but the movement is often inserted for the sake of enhancing the "real" learning. The implication is that if we can only get their blood pumping, the kids will better be able to learn X, Y, and Z.

But movement itself *is* learning, not just preparation for it. If our children are implicitly being taught through thirteen years of school that movement is an afterthought, we need to teach them explicitly how important it truly is. And to do that, we must be convinced ourselves.

We use the word "learning" as it pertains to movement throughout the course of many years. We speak of learning to crawl and learning to walk. Learning to swim, bike, and cast a fishing line are common milestones as well. But after these milestones—most of which occur during earlier childhood—are attained, we start to disassociate the word "learning" with movement, and it shifts to classroom knowledge. *She learned her multiplication tables. He learned how to write a five-paragraph essay.* We peel apart learning from movement right in our vernacular.

It's as if our language is missing words for any incremental steps beyond initial accomplishment. Those first adorable, unsure toddling steps look vastly different from a three-year-old careening through the woods, leaping over stumps, and running up and down embankments of various inclines. But we have incomplete language to speak of the differences, so these incremental yet monumental changes get lost in the shuffle. We don't talk about them enough, or at all. We live in a society, at least as far as school-aged children are concerned, where learning and bookwork are synonymous, and there are no gauges that measure, celebrate, or even take notice of the marvelous things that kids learn to do with their bodies.

When I speak at conferences, I tell a story of waterfall chasing in Asheville, North Carolina. I attempted to scamper after my kids at the base of the Second Falls at Graveyard Fields, a popular hiking trail along the Blue Ridge Parkway that got its name from some tree stumps that look like gravestones. The falls were roaring and powerful, and at their base were rocks submerged in shallow water, which allowed people to move around and see Second Falls from several vantage points.

This was an instance where skill level made a task look much easier than it actually was, like videos you may have seen of adults on playground equipment. Kids move seamlessly among the monkey bars, slides, and balance beams while the grown-ups fall and flail—a reminder of the competence of children.

The rocks along the base of Second Falls were covered in mosses and the type of film that builds up from submersion in constant rushing water. They were slick with an amount of variation we are rarely used to, rocks of different sizes and shapes that cut at different angles, some firmly rooted in position and others that tipped. I was immediately unsteady. Movement outdoors involves a brain component often missing from indoor exercise. I marveled at how quickly our young children moved through the maze, sure-footed and confident, while I fell farther and farther behind, giving great calculation to a single step.

Despite my caution, I slipped, and in the blink of an eye, our oldest daughter, who was only six at the time, had enough wherewithal in her body to thrust out an arm to steady me—a maneuver that my brain can't even fully grasp. She deemed it the vacation where she saved my life—an exaggeration, certainly, but a statement that carries with it the weight of the knowledge that sometimes kids are more competent than adults.

No matter where we are outside, nature provides the ultimate obstacle course because it is always changing. The 1000 Hours Outside movement is steeped in celebration. Families reach milestones and have cakes made or build their milestone number with seasonal natural materials. They will create a huge "800" out of leaf piles or a "250" using a unique arrangement of pumpkins. It is through this time outside, and especially when we go as a family, that we see firsthand the breadth of what our children are accomplishing. The complex movements that nature gently coaxes our children to try help enhance their cognition.

Our brains, filled with neurons, have room for one hundred trillion connections between those neurons. Amazingly, our neurons look an awful lot like trees. The center of a neuron, called the cell body or soma, is like the trunk. The axon, which is like one long cable running out from the soma, is like the tree roots. The five to seven dendrites that surround each neuron look like an array of tree branches, forming a beautiful canopy that envelops each neuron. In fact, *dendron* is the Greek word for "tree." Five to seven dendrites might not seem like much, but each of them can have tens of thousands of branches called dendritic spines. Dendrites receive and take information in toward the soma, and the axon carries information away from the soma.[2]

About 75 percent of the glorious dendrite canopy around each one of our unique neurons participates in synaptic transmission. Synapses, the small gaps between neurons by which an axon sends information to a receiving dendrite, allow neurons to pass electrical or chemical information to each other.

There is much to learn here that is beyond the scope of this book, but just as pruning a plant counterintuitively encourages growth, so too our brains prune synapses. At the same time, an insulating sheath called myelin is building up over the axon, and the thicker the sheath, the faster impulses can transmit. Brain imaging has allowed scientists to determine that intelligence is "strongly influenced by the quality of the brain's axons."[3]

You can think of myelin like forging a new trail. It is laid down with each subsequent excursion on the path. At the beginning, there are innumerable obstacles, so pushing ahead is slow going. The obstacles lie in front, below, and around and must be trampled or removed to increase speed. But with each additional jaunt down the trail, doing so becomes easier and faster. Repetition leads to myelination.

Well, what do young children do? They repeat. They try repeatedly. They learn a new skill and then lay down that pathway in their brain, nice and thick. It took over a year for our youngest daughter to learn to climb a fence. She would attempt, month after month, to get to the top and swing one leg over. Then she would call out for help because she couldn't make it over. When she finally figured out the mechanics to get down the other side, she repeated the process over and over again, each time with increasing speed and extra elements of bravery, like jumping from higher parts of the fence.

She did a similar thing on a random trip to a nearby museum as a toddler. In one section of the museum, there were two small steps that were separated by a large, flat carpeted area. Though we had other intentions for our visit to the museum, our daughter had her own lesson plans that day. Up and down she went over those two steps, time after time, internally motivated to master a skill.

Without any direction from guided lesson plans, our kids learn. The documentary *Babies*, directed by Thomas Balmès, follows the lives of four babies born in different parts of the world—Mongolia, Namibia, San Francisco, and Tokyo. Through the chronicling of their first years, you see the vast similarities in growth and development while simultaneously seeing expansive differences in environments. These four babies have lives set before them that will involve learning many unique things. Their own cultures, customs, languages, and brains are primed to adjust to an array of possibilities. Carla Hannaford puts it this way in her book *Smart Moves*: "We custom design our own nervous systems to meet the choice and challenges of our own interests and livelihoods."[4]

Our intelligence, our capacity to interact with the world, is dependent upon experiences, and yet we clutter a whopping portion of childhood with worksheets and sitting. In her book *Ready or Not*, Dr. Madeline Levine writes that though we want what's best for our children, the fear of an uncertain future is causing many of us to "double down on the old ways" that relied heavily on high grades and standardized test scores and had almost an assembly-line approach to them.[5] Set your child on the conveyor belt, incorporate these specific elements, follow an ordered sequence of instructions, and voilà! You've raised a superkid!

If you want to set your kids apart cognitively, do less. I know that is a terrifying proposition because it is unstructured, uncharted, and unpredictable, but it is a proven path. Underparenting, as opposed to overparenting, shells out the benefits. In open times and open spaces, especially in fresh air, benefits rain down on the child who is allowed to play freely.

So let them play, and more specifically, let them play outside when you can. Play is worthy of your time whenever and wherever it happens, but there's extra magic when it takes place outdoors. The increasingly complex movements kids engage in without your direction or supervision are helping them lay down a neural foundation that will enhance their life experience for their entire life. The outdoors offers unlimited potential for growth, and each season announces its arrival with new and enticing ways for children to participate.

The fall season sends kids to grab the rakes as they pull together pillowy piles of leaves that are ready for a leap and a land. There is endless delight in that which will decay and regenerate the earth while it sleeps. Pumpkins and gourds, with their myriad of sizes, shapes, and colors, can be carved into entire villages to play with. The push and pull on the joints that occur when the delights of autumn are lifted, carried, or pulled in a wagon help kids develop their proprioception sense.

Our bodies have proprioceptors, sensory receptors inside the body that transmit information about our joint activity, muscle tension, and equilibrium, giving us our sense of ourselves and where our body is located in space. The proprioception sense allows us to touch our nose or our foot with our eyes closed, and it's imperative for coordination and balance.

Winter serves up a new landscape for the proprioception sense. From snowballs to snow forts to snowmen to snow angels to snow lanterns to snowshoeing, what seems initially monotonous is inherently full of promise. The backdrop of white allows us to easily spot a cardinal in flight or a scampering chipmunk. The sound of cracking ice is alluring to kids of all ages as they smash it underfoot, and as that ice thickens, there is the thrilling challenge of remaining upright on a slippery surface. Constructing snow forts, simple shoveling, building snowmen, pushing and lifting those huge balls of snow, and even the trudge up a hill with a sled trailing behind are further opportunities to work on the proprioception sense. And when all the outdoor adventures are wrapped up, cozy comforts await indoors. The warmth from a crackling fire hits differently on hands and cheeks that have been chilled by the winter air. A bit of discomfort gives way to a greater sense of comfort.

Springtime draws us into the sunshine. Bodies parched for light and warmth emerge with everything else—flowers and baby animals. Awakening occurs simultaneously with a symphony of sights, sounds, and smells. There's mud to slide in and an anticipation that arrives with the awareness of lengthening days, gardens to begin, windows to fling open. Spring is synonymous with possibility, a time for rediscovery of the things that make us come alive. Will we return to the fishing hole? Pump air into our mountain bike tires? Break out the chalk for some artistic escapades? This is the time when, before the pesky insects arrive, we take strides to increase our endurance and stamina for all that is yet to come.

The summer, with its long and listless days, invites kids to press their bare toes into the sand, walking and maneuvering through a shifting surface beneath, one that works many different muscles of the legs and feet. With the warm sun on their backs, the sand beckons them to squat down and use the open-ended potential of the millions of grains surrounding them, as well as pieces of driftwood and buckets of water, to unleash their creativity with castles and moats, drawbridges, and rivers. Sending kids to collect firewood or allowing time to climb monkey bars or trees gives opportunities to again develop the proprioception sense.

An entire book could be written about the movement opportunities inherent in each season. It was Linda Akeson McGurk's book *There's No Such Thing as Bad Weather* that implored me to relish the distinctiveness of even the cold, wet, and dreary days.

When we want to give our kids every advantage as it pertains to academic standing, the year-round movements they partake in help them thrive in the classroom setting. It's the climbing and hanging, the digging and building, that get arms, shoulders, wrists, and fingers ready to write. It's the rough-and-tumble play that strengthens the core muscles, which are desperately needed for kids to be able to sit upright at a desk. It's the up-and-down motion that occurs as kids traipse down a trail that gives their eyes practice working together. The same thing happens for your toddler or baby when they are carried in a baby carrier. With each step, the eyes must work together to adjust the gaze, and all these minutes and hours add up, giving kids foundational physical skills that will assist them with reading.

Time in nature gives children a chance to test their outer limits and often go beyond them. The environment is perfectly conducive to grappling with perceived capability and figuring out how to live within that or to push beyond it. The things kids learn in nature about themselves are life skills. Not only are they learning *how* to learn, but they are also learning how thrilling growth is. Something new awaits beyond this skill. Their curiosities beckon them on.

Learning to Risk

MasterClass is a platform that streams video lessons taught by the best of the best from around the world and includes categories like cooking, acting, writing, photography, business, sports, and more. Jimmy Chin, National Geographic photographer and filmmaker, teaches a course through MasterClass called "Adventure Photography." Who even knew there was such a thing? The course covers the basics that many photography courses do—things like focal length, aperture, and how to deal with sun flares. But you know this class is going to have a twist when, right in the trailer, Chin says, "Things aren't that interesting to me unless the stakes are very high,"[6] and images of ski slopes, mountain peaks, and vast expanses ensue. Chin's claim to fame is not only his stunning photography that tells a story but the lengths at which he goes to get the image. As a part of this course, he goes beyond the photo and touches on risk in a lesson called "High-Stakes Photography."

Not only does he touch on risk, but he presents it as a calculation that can be extended into all walks of life, drawn out and thought through. For the sake of determining risk when it comes to outdoor play, the mind often works like a lightning bolt. Chin enlightens us on the risk equation: consequence × probability = risk. In other words, a high-consequence activity that carries with it a high likelihood of occurring is extremely risky. An example would be letting a young child play with a ball near a busy intersection with lots of traffic under no adult supervision. It's an incredibly risky move because the consequences could be disastrous and the likelihood of something happening is also high. However, letting a young child play in a grassy field with a ball is hardly risky as the consequence and probability are low. Playing with a ball on a stretch of cement would fall somewhere in between.

The question that arises is not how risky a particular scenario is, but rather, who should the assessor be? Who should carry the role as primary risk mathematician, mentally computing and making the calls?

Maybe one of the largest and most impactful generational changes to have occurred in the last fifty years is that children, after the toddler and preschool years, used to make a majority of their own risk calculations, but in a well-intentioned pursuit of safety, we as parents have mistakenly demanded the calculator. And we rarely hand it back. I say "mistakenly" because our choice to be the primary decision-maker creates kids who are less safe in the long run. What was happening during all those years when kids played until the streetlights came on? They were calculating. *How dangerous is this? How likely is it to happen?* Over and over again, they had the opportunity to explore their own bandwidths, and determining personal capacity became second nature.

We are too focused on what we can offer our kids instead of considering what our kids have to offer themselves. When we allow them to be unsupervised in age-appropriate ways outdoors, we are giving them familiarity. They are learning their bodies and their surroundings. We are learning in small increments how to let go.

We think of childhood as a time for the child, its length being considerably greater than the development time of all other mammals, and we conclude it is because the child needs a certain number of years for growth before adulthood. But maybe its length is meant for us too—a slow, drawn-out release of the reins, a letting go that lasts over a period of many years, a transferring of the relay baton, slowed down to imperceptible movements. Forgetting ourselves results in a repeated mantra of "they need, they need, they need." But what do we need? We need to let them fly and then be their loudest cheering section. How can we release if we don't know what they are capable of, if we haven't seen their innate capacity to take their own lives and advance them forward?

Some would say this time in nature is optional. *It's too cold. The mosquitos are too bad. The mud will get everywhere. We don't have the time. There's too much on my plate. My kids don't want to go.* Yet risk assessment is a skill set, and new skills are learned through doing. How many opportunities truly exist indoors for kids to get the practice they need to test their limits? How well are we stretched in our capacity to launch another human—our most precious possession—into a harsh and unsteady world when we spend much of our time surrounded by carpet and sofas? Where will the grit come from? And the resilience, the tenacity, the flexibility, and the stamina? From our air conditioners? The world our kids will cross a threshold into will not surround them in a bubble. Their paths will not be straight and set before them. There will be struggles, hard decisions, doubt, fear, uncertainty, disappointment, sadness, anger, confusion, frustration, and hostility, with immense joy interlaced through all of it. Does an inside world, an indoor childhood, adequately prepare them for their futures? And for our own futures when we can no longer be at arm's length?

I took my kids to a local pool once, and after I had paid, everyone changed into life jackets per the rules and entered the pool, only to be told by the lifeguard on duty that I had to always be within arm's reach of my kids. That would've been good information to know prior to paying and finagling everyone into bathing suits, seeing as how I had four kids at the time yet only two arms. I understood the legality of it, but I also had a firm grasp on which of our four children were strong swimmers and which ones needed more assistance. I could've safely and securely navigated our one-hour swim slot in the shallow area of the pool without the go-go-gadget-arms rule.

This reminded me of our society at large. It's as if we want no risk at all. Consequences lurk at every street corner, on metal slides, and in just a few inches of water. We cannot control the consequences, so we've decided to aim for zero probability. Go back to the equation. If probability is zero, then so is risk because zero times anything is zero. Zero probability means no risk at all, but what kind of life would that be? One that is primed and ready for the metaverse, perhaps?

What Counts as Being Outside?

The question I get asked most often about the 1000 Hours Outside movement is "Does sleeping in a tent count as hours outside?" I'm going to leave you hanging with that one because we have no official rules. Still, the "does it count" questions come in fast and furious. Can we count the time we are driving to an outdoor space? What if our windows are down? What if we're in a convertible? Does time in a stroller count? Time in a cave? What if my kids are outside but they're playing inside cardboard boxes?

The thing about time in nature is that even if we don't move much—even if we want to shed the idea of risky and take the safer path for now, giving ourselves time to work into a braver disposition—we still get benefits, and lots of them. If we take a meal outside, play card games on the porch, or read a book with our backs up against a tree trunk, we do a lot for ourselves and our children. Amazingly, there are still those tremendous benefits that come in the form of full-spectrum light exposure, as well as the surround sounds, the aromatic smells, and the world of things to see that nature provides.

When time is limited, our immediate outdoor surroundings aren't accessible, or our knees are shaky for whatever reason, nature still provides, and our circumstances don't have to be ideal in order to glean the benefits. Even bringing elements of nature indoors has the potential to impact our family or our classroom. Enjoying nature inside can be as simple as having a windowsill herb garden, a bathtub filled with snow, or a glob of homemade Play-Doh filled with wildflower petals. It doesn't have to be perfect; it just has to be something.

My story of a life changed by nature time began simply on a picnic blanket. And to this day, well over a decade later, it continues in a similar fashion. The day I met up with my friend from MOPS, the day that I was convinced would be sheer pandemonium (for four hours straight), ended up being a transformative experience that took the course of my parenting and the path of our family in a different direction in an instant. Nature handed me the reprieve I was seeking—immediately—and it has continued to be dependable ever since. Nature never stops working as a balm for emotions, as a location for our betterment, as a place for our wildest adventures, and as a help to our parenting.

I got a text from a friend today. It was filled with doubt, spewing the looming question we all ask: "Am I doing enough?" It's a desperate scream that lives within our souls. We attempt to hush the noise, but it squeezes out into doubts and insecurities. What can we do but live fully today? What can we do but take the time that is at our fingertips, the right now, and live the life out of it?

Set down your phones. Run barefoot through the grass. Let snowflakes land on your cheeks. Break out a deck of cards on the deck. Lean in. Listen. Relax. Smile. Enjoy. Toss the baseball until the streetlights come on, and then watch the stars appear. You're doing enough. Keep going. It's the small things that add up to a big life.

Discussion Questions

1. What were your favorite outdoor movements as a child?
2. As you age, do you continue to move in ways that challenge your body?
3. How does movement affect learning?

Action and Adventure Prompts

1. Try to move in a way that is a little more complicated than you're used to this week.
2. Observe the progression of movement in your children when they're given time and space to play in nature.
3. Play outside until the streetlights come on.

Conclusion

A conclusion feels so final, like I'm wrapping a beautiful bow on a finished present, but the reality is I have stacks of books and research that remain unread. I fear that I left something out, something life changing, something pertinent. That must be the case, as there is always more to be learned. This is not a culmination; it is a reflection.

We don't get to write books in the after. We write them in the during. This is forty-two years of contemplation, where more than half my days have been spent in adulthood and exactly a third of them in the role of mom. But I still have a long way to go.

The message of my soul is this: If I could go back in time and do this whole parenting thing all over again, I wouldn't change a thing. I'd leave the dirty dishes and the dusty baseboards every single time for the sake of strapping a baby to my front and a toddler to my back so we could head down a trail and have a picnic lunch underneath a tree. I'd scrap the schoolwork until the ages you start to get judged so we could play in the dirt and collect sticks. I'd build the friendships knowing not all of them would last and there would be times we'd show up and be the only ones.

We are struggling as humans with life satisfaction, with fear, with disconnectedness. Because we are so smart and sophisticated and have access to the World Wide Web in our pockets, we look for the calculus-level answers to our daily problems when we may not need something so complicated.

A look back to the years when kids played unsupervised until the streetlights came on is healthy and necessary. It's good to remember where we came from. Not all of it was perfect, but hindsight allows us to pick and choose. If that was your era, select some of the good parts and try to re-create them. If it was before your time, ask around. What was it like for the kids, the parents, and the educators to live among childhood play?

Once you've looked back, look at your now. Really look. You've come this far. You should be so proud. Today is the day when you get to choose how you want your family to be.

If you need continued inspiration and encouragement, head over to 1000HoursOutside.com, where we offer time-tracking sheets, yearly kickoff packs with monthly adventure prompts, and all sorts of outdoor gear for your family. We also have a number-one mobile app for iOS and Android called "1000 Hours Outside," with a timer feature and milestone badges you can earn; a highly engaged and growing private Facebook group; and a top-ranked podcast called *The 1000 Hours Outside Podcast.* The list of guests is long and distinguished, and many of them have dedicated their lives to the betterment of childhood.

Acknowledgments

Josh, I love you. I love adventuring with you, whether it's big or small. Trails, books, businesses, waterfalls, raising a family, conferences, and walks around the neighborhood. There's no one else I'd rather do it all with.

Jackson, thanks for being such a strong, dependable son . . . and also for bringing me MichiMinis. You're a great kid with a lot of heart, vision, hard work, and wisdom, and I love being your mom.

Vivian, thanks for serenading me with your beautiful guitar playing while I wrote. Your talent makes my head spin. I love our late-night talks. What a gift and honor to be your mom and friend.

Charlie, thanks for playing Azul with me when I needed a break from writing and for being such a loving bruh. I couldn't ask for a better middle-of-the-pack. Being your mom is so much fun!

Brooklyn, thanks for adding your stylish flair to our family. You always make me smile. You're such a good friend. I'm thankful for your incredible big-sister vibes, and I'm so glad I'm your mom.

Winnie Jo, thanks for drawing 892 pictures of me while I wrote this book. I'm a huge fan of your artwork. Thanks for being patient and understanding while I worked. Being your mom is amazing!

Bubby and Zeydie, you are a dream come true. Thanks for enthusiastically spreading the message of 1000 Hours Outside by wearing the T-shirts and using the water bottles. You mean the world to all of us.

Nana and Papa, thanks for being delightful and encouraging in all our crazy endeavors. We love you to the moon and back!

To both sets of grandparents, we cherish all the outdoor memories we've shared together—and there are so many beautiful ones! Thanks for being such attentive, intentional, involved, and loving grandparents. We hit the jackpot with you!

Carrot Day friends, our bonds along with the ones our children share helped keep me loving life throughout this writing process. I love each of you deeply and dearly. Long live Carrot Day!

Beth, you are my rock—always dependable and always there with an endless well of wisdom and encouragement. You've enhanced my life more than words can say. Love you!

Missie, you have given me a vision for family life well into adulthood. Thanks for inviting us into your family, where we've gotten a front-row seat to see things like cousin week and all the ways you invest in experiences. And wow, your hair is lovely.

Suzanne, this one's for you. It's finally here! I've been tickled from the very beginning by the interest you've shown. Thanks for being an integral part of this journey.

Rachel Jacobson, you have changed my life and my family's lives in ways we don't even know yet. I am forever grateful. You are remarkably talented at what you do, and I look forward to the years to come.

To the entire Baker team, I can't say how much I appreciate you all. I have loved working with each of you and am already looking forward to what's next! Special thanks to Rebekah, Olivia, Eileen, Laura, Holly, and Jessica for your outstanding help from start to finish. This is an opportunity of a lifetime, and the whole experience has been beyond a thrill! Thank you for all of it.

Daniel Neuman, your creative aesthetic is truly one of a kind, and I'm so inspired by what you do. Thanks for being a significant part of the 1000 Hours Outside movement.

To all the *1000 Hours Outside Podcast* guests, thank you for your wisdom, knowledge, kind words, and time. You've impacted my own life in immeasurable ways, and your deep insights have reached millions.

To the entire 1000 Hours Outside global community, everyone says you are the best community, and it's the truth. You are always encouraging, always enthusiastic, and always brilliant with your ideas. Keep going! What you're doing matters.

Notes

Introduction

1. Jerry Kaplan, *Humans Need Not Apply: A Guide to Wealth and Work in the Age of Artificial Intelligence* (New Haven, CT: Yale University Press, 2016), 44.

Chapter 1 A Great Divide

1. Ginny Yurich and Thomas Kersting, "Multitasking Reduces Cognitive Capacity to That of an Eight-Year-Old," September 30, 2021, in *The 1000 Hours Outside Podcast*, produced by Open Air Productions, https://podcasts.apple.com/us/podcast/the-1000-hours-outside-podcast/id1448210728?i=1000537122388.

2. Ginny Yurich and Angela Hanscom, "Play Is the Main Occupation of Childhood," November 4, 2021, in *The 1000 Hours Outside Podcast*, produced by Open Air Productions, https://podcasts.apple.com/us/podcast/the-1000-hours-outside-podcast/id1448210728?i=1000540738625.

3. Yurich and Hanscom, "Play Is the Main Occupation."

4. Ginny Yurich and Nicholas Kardaras, "How to Compete with the Stimulation of Screens," January 20, 2022, in *The 1000 Hours Outside Podcast*, produced by Open Air Productions, https://podcasts.apple.com/us/podcast/the-1000-hours-outside-podcast/id1448210728?i=1000548464807.

5. Susan Linn, *The Case for Make Believe: Saving Play in a Commercialized World* (New York: The New Press, 2008), 13.

6. Nicholas Kardaras, *Glow Kids: How Screen Addiction Is Hijacking Our Kids—and How to Break the Trance* (New York: St. Martin's Griffin, 2017), 30.

7. Kardaras, *Glow Kids*, 218.

8. Cal Newport, *Digital Minimalism: Choosing a Focused Life in a Noisy World* (New York: Penguin LLC, 2019), 130.

9. Kardaras, *Glow Kids*, 23.

10. Ginny Yurich and Kim John Payne, "The Undeclared War on Childhood," February 17, 2022, in *The 1000 Hours Outside Podcast*, produced by Open Air Productions, https://podcasts.apple.com/us/podcast/the -1000-hours-outside-podcast/id1448210728?i=1000551379827.

11. Jay Donovan, "The Average Age for a Child Getting Their First Smartphone Is Now 10.3 Years," Tech Crunch, May 19, 2016, https://tech crunch.com/2016/05/19/the-average-age-for-a-child-getting-their-first -smartphone-is-now-10-3-years.

12. Ginny Yurich and Dr. Peter Gray, "When School Wasn't Such a Big Deal," September 16, 2021, in *The 1000 Hours Outside Podcast*, produced by Open Air Productions, https://podcasts.apple.com/us/podcast /the-1000-hours-outside-podcast/id1448210728?i=1000535528011.

13. Gary R. Edgerton, *The Columbia History of American Television* (New York: Columbia University Press, 2009), xi.

14. Winifred Gallagher, *New: Understanding Our Need for Novelty and Change* (New York: Penguin Press, 2011), 159.

15. Yurich and Kardaras, "How to Compete."

16. "There's a Reason They Call It the Great Outdoors," National Wildlife Federation, 2010, https://www.nwf.org/~/media/PDFs/Be%20Out %20There/MindBodySpirit_FactSheet_May2010.ashx.

17. Kaplan, *Humans Need Not Apply*, 28.

18. Andy Crouch, *The Tech-Wise Family: Everyday Steps for Putting Technology in Its Proper Place* (Grand Rapids: Baker Books, 2017), 17.

19. Neil Postman, *The Disappearance of Childhood* (New York: Vintage Books, 1994), 71.

20. Roger Bohn and James Short, "How Much Information?: 2009 Report on American Consumers," Global Information Industry Center, 2009, https://group47.com/HMI_2009_ConsumerReport_Dec9_2009 .pdf.

21. Roger Bohn and James Short, "Measuring Consumer Information," *International Journal of Communication* 6 (2012), https://ijoc .org/index.php/ijoc/article/viewFile/1566/743.

22. Greg Lukianoff, *The Coddling of the American Mind: How Good Intentions and Bad Ideas Are Setting Up a Generation for Failure* (New York: Penguin Press, 2018), 187.

23. Postman, *The Disappearance of Childhood*, 46.

24. Tom Hobson, *Teacher Tom's Second Book: Teaching and Learning from Preschoolers* (Seattle: Peanut Butter Publishing, 2020), 103.

25. Kim John Payne with Lisa M. Ross, *Simplicity Parenting: Using the Extraordinary Power of Less to Raise Calmer, Happier, and More Secure Kids* (New York: Ballantine Books, 2009), 83.

26. Praneeth Palli, "'Humans Will Live in Metaverse Soon,' Claims Mark Zuckerberg. What about Reality?," Mashable India, March 4, 2022, https://in.mashable.com/tech/28254/humans-will-live-in-metaverse-soon-claims-mark-zuckerberg-what-about-reality.

27. Kardaras, *Glow Kids*, 89.

28. Kardaras, *Glow Kids*, 219.

Chapter 2 Slow Down and Gain More

1. Kaplan, *Humans Need Not Apply*, 150.

2. Sebastian Anthony, "Researchers Create Fiber Network That Operates at 99.7% Speed of Light, Smashes Speed and Latency Records," Extreme Tech, March 25, 2013, https://www.extremetech.com/science/151498-researchers-create-fiber-network-that-operates-at-99-7-speed-of-light-smashes-speed-and-latency-records.

3. "Youth Indicators 2011: America's Youth: Transitions to Adulthood," National Center for Education Statistics, December 2011, https://nces.ed.gov/pubs2012/2012026/tables/table_35.asp.

4. Simon Sinek, *The Infinite Game* (London, United Kingdom: Penguin Random House UK, 2019), 4.

5. "Original Quotes and Favorite Sayings from Magda Gerber," Magda Gerber Legacy, accessed April 25, 2023, https://magdagerber.org/magda-gerber-quotes.

6. "Tom Stoppard Quotes," Goodreads, accessed April 25, 2023, https://www.goodreads.com/quotes/29024-because-children-grow-up-we-think-a-child-s-purpose-is.

7. "Lillian Dickson Quotes," All Great Quotes, accessed April 25, 2023, https://www.allgreatquotes.com/only-spend-it-once.

8. Linda Flanagan, *Take Back the Game: How Money and Mania Are Ruining Kids' Sports—and Why It Matters* (New York: Portfolio, 2022), 48.

9. Michael Luca and Jonathan Smith, "Salience in Quality Disclosure: Evidence from the U.S. News College Rankings," Leadership and Management Articles, September 27, 2011, https://web.archive.org/web/20131107041503/http://leadershiparticles.info/2011/09/salience-in-quality-disclosure-evidence-from-the-u-s-news-college-rankings.

10. Flanagan, *Take Back the Game*, 48.

11. Flanagan, *Take Back the Game*, 48.

12. Xavier Blackwell-Lipkind, "Feature: 'Gray Area': College Admissions and the Private Counseling Machine," *Yale Daily News*, May 10,

2019, https://yaledailynews.com/blog/2021/04/29/feature-gray-area-college-admissions-and-the-private-counseling-machine.

13. "What Receiving College Brochures Means," *Ivy Coach* (blog), October 17, 2017, https://www.ivycoach.com/the-ivy-coach-blog/college-admissions/receiving-college-brochures-means/.

14. Linda McGurk, *There's No Such Thing as Bad Weather: A Scandinavian Mom's Secrets for Raising Healthy, Resilient, and Confident Kids (from Friluftsliv to Hygge)* (New York: Touchstone, 2018), 43.

15. Shirag Shemmassian, "Is Attending an Ivy League Worth It? The Real Benefits of an Ivy League Education," Shemmassian Academic Consulting, accessed April 25, 2023, https://www.shemmassianconsulting.com/blog/is-ivy-league-worth-it.

16. Payne, *Simplicity Parenting*, 152.

17. Carla Hannaford, *The Dominance Factor: How Knowing Your Dominant Eye, Ear, Brain, Hand & Foot Can Improve Your Learning* (Salt Lake City: Great River Books, 2011), 126.

18. John Taylor Gatto, *Dumbing Us Down: The Hidden Curriculum of Compulsory Education* (Gabriola, British Columbia: New Society Publishers, 2017), 11.

19. Ginny Yurich and Carla Hannaford, "We Cannot Learn Sitting Still and Being Quiet," February 6, 2023, in *The 1000 Hours Outside Podcast*, produced by Open Air Productions, https://podcasts.apple.com/us/podcast/the-1000-hours-outside-podcast/id1448210728?i=1000598257423.

20. Hannaford, *The Dominance Factor*, 128.

21. "Why Do Fluorescent Lights Make You Feel Weird?," *Make Great Light* (blog), October 19, 2021, https://www.makegreatlight.com/about-us/blog/fluorescent-lights-causing-weird-feeling.

22. Ginny Yurich and Kim John Payne, "We Underestimate the Power of Family," August 10, 2022, in *The 1000 Hours Outside Podcast*, produced by Open Air Productions, https://podcasts.apple.com/us/podcast/the-1000-hours-outside-podcast/id1448210728?i=1000575715229.

23. Kaplan, *Humans Need Not Apply*, 4.

24. Kaplan, *Humans Need Not Apply*, 13.

Chapter 3 Rescue Childhood and Save Your Sanity

1. Kardaras, *Glow Kids*, 127.

2. "At-Home Learning," VTech, accessed April 25, 2023, https://www.vtechkids.com/homelearning.

3. "Level Up Gaming Chair," VTech, accessed April 25, 2023, https://www.vtechkids.com/product/detail/20347/Level_Up_Gaming_Chair.

4. Linn, *The Case for Make Believe*, 4.

5. "Go on a Learning Adventure," LeapFrog Academy, accessed April 25, 2023, https://store.leapfrog.com/en-us/academy/landing.

6. "My First Kidi Smartwatch," VTech, accessed April 25, 2023, https://www.vtechkids.com/product/detail/20337/My_First_Kidi_Smartwatch.

7. Linn, *The Case for Make Believe*, 57.

8. Minigran Wang, "Mattel's Earning Surprise Shows Compelling Value in VTech," Seeking Alpha, July 27, 2020, https://seekingalpha.com/article/4361097-mattels-earnings-surprise-shows-compelling-value-in-vtech.

9. Anya Kamenetz and Elissa Nadworny, "More Testing, Less Play: Study Finds Higher Expectations for Kindergartners," NPR, June 21, 2016, https://www.npr.org/sections/ed/2016/06/21/481404169/more-testing-less-play-study-finds-higher-expectations-for-kindergartners.

10. Scott Barry Kaufman, *Ungifted: Intelligence Redefined* (New York: Basic Books, 2015), xx.

11. Jon Acuff with L.E. Acuff and McRae Acuff, *Your New Playlist: The Student's Guide to Tapping into the Superpower of Mindset* (Grand Rapids: Baker Books, 2022), 65.

12. Lana Stenner, *The Grace-Filled Homestead: Lessons I've Learned about Faith, Family, and the Farm* (Eugene, OR: Ten Peaks Press, 2022), 47.

13. Michael Easter, *The Comfort Crisis: Embrace Discomfort to Reclaim Your Wild, Happy, Healthy Self* (Emmaus, PA: Rodale Books, 2021), 76.

14. Ginny Yurich and Jon Acuff, "I Want My Family to Get the Best of Me, Not the Rest of Me," September 13, 2022, in *The 1000 Hours Outside Podcast*, produced by Open Air Productions, https://podcasts.apple.com/us/podcast/the-1000-hours-outside-podcast/id1448210728?i=1000579315329.

Chapter 4 Bored to Tears

1. Johann Hari, *Stolen Focus: Why You Can't Pay Attention—and How to Think Deeply Again* (New York: Crown, 2022), 96.

2. Scott Sampson, *How to Raise a Wild Child: The Art and Science of Falling in Love with Nature* (Boston: Mariner Books, 2016), 14.

3. Michael Rucker, *The Fun Habit: How the Pursuit of Joy and Wonder Can Change Your Life* (New York: Atria Books, 2023), 35.

4. George Land, "Dr. George Land: The Failure of Success," YouTube video, posted by "TEDx Talks," February 16, 2011, https://youtu.be/ZfKMq-rYtnc.

5. Austin Kleon, "The Trouble with Being Lazy," *Austin Kleon* (blog), May 10, 2019, https://austinkleon.com/2019/05/10/the-trouble-with-being-lazy.

6. Newport, *Digital Minimalism*, 92.

7. Easter, *The Comfort Crisis*, 116.

8. Easter, *The Comfort Crisis*, 116.

9. Austin Kleon, *Steal Like an Artist: 10 Things Nobody Told You about Being Creative* (New York: Workman Publishing Company, 2012), 61.

10. Ray Kurzweil, *The Singularity Is Near: When Humans Transcend Biology* (New York: Penguin Group, 2006), 309.

11. Richard Louv, *Last Child in the Woods: Saving Our Children from Nature-Deficit Disorder* (Chapel Hill: Algonquin Books, 2008), 7.

12. Easter, *The Comfort Crisis*, 13.

13. Rucker, *The Fun Habit*, 34.

14. Newport, *Digital Minimalism*, 115.

15. "Henry David Thoreau Quotes," Goodreads, accessed April 25, 2023, https://www.goodreads.com/quotes/8202-the-mass-of-men-lead-lives-of-quiet-desperation-what.

Chapter 5 Good Day, Sunshine

1. E. M. Tam, R. W. Lam, and A. J. Levitt, "Treatment of Seasonal Affective Disorder: A Review," PubMed, October 1995, https://pubmed.ncbi.nlm.nih.gov/8681269.

2. Ginny Yurich and Jacob Liberman, "Every Function of Your Body Is Continually Responding to Nature. Learn about the Power of Full Spectrum Sunlight with Dr. Jacob Liberman," October 14, 2021, in *The 1000 Hours Outside Podcast*, produced by Open Air Productions, https://podcasts.apple.com/us/podcast/the-1000-hours-outside-podcast/id1448210728?i=1000538573867.

3. Sara Goudarzi, "Everyone's Eyes Are Wired Differently," NBC News, November 28, 2005, https://www.nbcnews.com/id/wbna10239783.

4. Jared Minkel and David F. Dinges, "Circadian Rhythms in Sleepiness, Alertness, and Performance," Science Direct, November 5, 2008, https://www.sciencedirect.com/science/article/pii/B9780080450469016223?via%3Dihub.

5. Merrill M. Mitler et. al, "Catastrophes, Sleep, and Public Policy: Consensus Report," National Library of Medicine, February 1988, https://www.ncbi.nlm.nih.gov/pmc/articles/PMC2517096.

6. Gail M. Morris, Christopher Kline, and Scott M. Morris, "Status of *Danaus Plexippus* Population in Arizona," BioOne Digital Library, June 1, 2015, https://bioone.org/journals/the-journal-of-the-lepidopterists-society/volume-69/issue-2/lepi.69i2.a10/Status-of-Danaus-plexippus-Population-in-Arizona/10.18473/lepi.69i2.a10.full.

7. "Why Support IDA?," International Dark-Sky Association, accessed April 25, 2023, https://www.darksky.org/why-support-ida.

8. Payne, *Simplicity Parenting*, 103.

9. "How to Eat: Diet Secrets from Michael Pollan (and Your Great-Grandma)," *Houston Chronicle*, January 23, 2010, https://michaelpollan.com/reviews/how-to-eat.

10. Anadi Martel, *Light Therapies: A Complete Guide to the Healing Power of Light* (Rochester, VT: Healing Arts Press, 2018), 23.

11. Quoted in Jacob Liberman, *Light: Medicine of the Future* (Rochester, VT: Bear & Company, 1991), 8.

12. Neil E. Klepeis et al., "The National Human Activity Pattern Survey (NHAPS): A Resource for Assessing Exposure to Environmental Pollutants," *Journal of Exposure Science & Environmental Epidemiology* 11 (July 26, 2001), https://www.nature.com/articles/7500165.

13. "Screen Time vs. Lean Time Infographic," Center for Disease Control and Prevention, accessed April 25, 2023, https://www.cdc.gov/nccd php/dnpao/multimedia/infographics/getmoving.html.

14. Rick Ansorge, "13 Tips to Prevent Eye Fatigue," WebMD, February 21, 2023, https://www.webmd.com/eye-health/eye-fatigue-causes-symp toms-treatment.

15. Fox Van Allen, "Doctor Warns: Smartphones Are Causing an Eye Epidemic," Techlicious, August 19, 2013, https://www.techlicious.com /blog/doctor-warns-smartphones-are-causing-an-eye-epidemic.

16. "Myopia: A Close Look at Efforts to Turn Back a Growing Problem," National Eye Institute, October 3, 2017, https://www.nei.nih.gov /about/news-and-events/news/myopia-close-look-efforts-turn-back-grow ing-problem.

17. Zane Kime, quoted in Liberman, *Light*, 10.

Chapter 6 There's a Lid for Every Pot

1. Shannan Martin, *Start with Hello: (And Other Simple Ways to Live as Neighbors)* (Grand Rapids: Revell, 2022), 30.

2. Payne, *Simplicity Parenting*, 83.

3. Dale Carnegie, *How to Win Friends and Influence People* (New York: Pocket Books, 1981), 93.

4. Peter Gray, *Free to Learn: Why Unleashing the Instinct to Play Will Make Our Children Happier, More Self-Reliant, and Better Students for Life* (New York: Basic Books, 2013), 167.

5. Gray, *Free to Learn*, 157.

6. Jean Twenge, *iGen: Why Today's Super-Connected Kids Are Growing Up Less Rebellious, More Tolerant, Less Happy—and Completely Unprepared for Adulthood—and What That Means for the Rest of Us* (New York: Simon & Schuster, 2018), 69.

7. Lenore Skenazy, *Free-Range Kids: How Parents and Teachers Can Let Go and Let Grow* (Hoboken, NJ: Jossey-Bass, 2021), 136.

8. Skenazy, *Free-Range Kids*, xxii.

9. Twenge, *iGen*, 96.

10. Twenge, *iGen*, 78.

11. Julianne Holt-Lunstad et al., "Loneliness and Social Isolation as Risk Factors for Mortality: A Meta-Analytic Review," *Sage Journals* 10, no. 2 (March 11, 2015), https://journals.sagepub.com/doi/abs/10.1177 /1745691614568352?journalCode=ppsa.

12. Crouch, *The Tech-Wise Family*, 157.

13. Wait Until 8th, accessed April 25, 2023, https://www.waituntil8th .org.

14. Todd Wilson, *How to Choose Relationship When There's So Much to Do* (Milford, IN: The Smiling Homeschooler, 2020), 51.

15. Kim John Payne, *Being Your Best When Your Kids Are at Their Worst: Practical Compassion in Parenting* (Boulder, CO: Shambhala Publications, 2019), 22.

16. Kristen A. Jenson, "Collin Kartchner: 11 Ways to #SavetheKids and Honor His Memory," Defend Young Minds, October 30, 2020, https:// www.defendyoungminds.com/post/collin-kartchner-11-ways-savethekids -honor-his-memory.

Chapter 7 The Art of Building a Family

1. Ruth Hulburt Hamilton, "Song for a Fifth Child," Rev. Joe Horn's personal website, accessed April 25, 2023, http://holyjoe.org/poetry/ham ilton.htm.

2. "Average Number of Own Children under 18 in Families with Children in the United States from 1960 to 2022," Statista, accessed April 25, 2023, https://www.statista.com/statistics/718084/average-number-of -own-children-per-family.

3. Hamilton, "Song for a Fifth Child."

4. Wilson, *How to Choose Relationship*, 5.

5. Ginny Yurich and Jon Acuff, "How to Make It Past Quitter's Day," January 9, 2023, in *The 1000 Hours Outside Podcast*, produced by Open Air Productions, https://podcasts.apple.com/us/podcast/the-1000-hours -outside-podcast/id1448210728?i=1000593094687.

6. "Toys and Games Market Size, Share & Trends Analysis Report by Product (Preschool Toys, Dolls), by Application (0–8 Years, 15 Years & Above), by Distribution Channel (Offline, Online), by Region, and Segment Forecasts, 2022–2030," Grand View Research, accessed April 25, 2023, https://www.grandviewresearch.com/industry-analysis/toys -games-market.

7. "Salesforce Live: Tristan Harris on How to Stop Technology from Destabilizing the World," Center for Humane Technology, September 25, 2018, https://www.humanetech.com/news/how-to-stop-technology -from-destabilizing-the-world.

8. Kardaras, *Glow Kids*, 18.

9. Nicholas Kardaras, *Digital Madness: How Social Media Is Driving Our Mental Health Crisis—and How to Restore Our Sanity* (New York: St. Martin's Press, 2022), 41.

10. Daniel Ruby, "26+ iPhone User & Sales Statistics (Fresh Data 2023)," Demand Sage, February 3, 2023, https://www.demandsage.com/iphone-user-statistics.

11. Payne, *Simplicity Parenting*, 165.

12. Flanagan, *Take Back the Game*, 83.

13. Flanagan, *Take Back the Game*, 184.

14. Flanagan, *Take Back the Game*, 74.

15. Kaufman, *Ungifted*, 219.

16. Kim John Payne, Luis Fernando Llosa, and Scott Lancaster, *Beyond Winning: Smart Parenting in a Toxic Sports Environment* (Guilford, CT: Lyons Press, 2013), 74.

17. David Elkind, *Miseducation: Preschoolers at Risk* (New York: Knopf, 1987), 192.

18. Madeline Levine, *Ready or Not: Preparing Our Kids to Thrive in an Uncertain and Rapidly Changing World* (New York: Harper Perennial, 2020), xix.

19. Levine, *Ready or Not*, 5.

20. Levine, *Ready or Not*, xix.

21. Ainsley Arment, *The Wild + Free Family: Forging Your Own Path to a Life Full of Wonder, Adventure, and Connection* (New York: HarperOne, 2022), 11.

22. David K. Johnson, "Ray Kurzweil's Crazy Yet Somewhat Precise Predictions about the Future," Wondrium Daily, June 1, 2021, https://www.wondriumdaily.com/ray-kurzweils-crazy-yet-somewhat-precise-predictions-about-the-future.

23. Kurzweil, *The Singularity Is Near*, 8–9.

24. Kurzweil, *The Singularity Is Near*, 9.

25. Kardaras, *Digital Madness*, 17.

26. Kurzweil, *The Singularity Is Near*, 341.

27. Kurzweil, *The Singularity Is Near*, 342.

28. "The Link," Neuralink, accessed April 25, 2023, https://neuralink.com/approach.

29. Kardaras, *Digital Madness*, 186.

30. Neil Postman, *Amusing Ourselves to Death: Public Discourse in the Age of Show Business* (New York: Penguin Group, 1985), xix.

31. Postman, *Amusing Ourselves to Death*, 161.

32. Kurzweil, *The Singularity Is Near*, 4.

33. "About Tristan," Tristan Harris (website), accessed April 25, 2023, https://www.tristanharris.com/#about.

34. Michelle Codiva, "Bill Gates Supports Climate-Smart Magic Seeds to Fight Global Hunger," The Science Times, September 15, 2022, https://www.sciencetimes.com/articles/39938/20220915/bill-gates-supports-climate-smart-magic-seeds-fight-global-hunger.htm.

35. Carmine Gallo, "Bill Gates Says Steve Jobs 'Cast Spells' on His Audience During Presentations. Here Are 3 Ways the Apple Wizard Worked His Magic," Inc., July, 10, 2019, https://www.inc.com/carmine-gallo/bill-gates-says-steve-jobs-cast-spells-on-his-audience-during-presentations-here-are-3-ways-apple-wizard-worked-his-magic.html.

Chapter 8 I Don't Remember the Quadratic Formula

1. Rich Karlgaard, *Late Bloomer: The Hidden Strengths of Learning and Succeeding at Your Own Pace* (New York: Broadway Books, 2019), 136.

2. Ainsley Arment, *The Call of the Wild + Free: Reclaiming Wonder in Your Child's Education* (New York: HarperOne, 2019), 293.

3. Allison Brooke Morgan, "Bowen Family Systems Theory in the Life and Works of Ernest Hemingway" (honors thesis, University of Mississippi, 2007), 25, https://egrove.olemiss.edu/hon_thesis/2382.

4. Alison Flood, "Ray Bradbury Rides Out in Defense of Libraries," *The Guardian*, June 22, 2009, https://www.theguardian.com/books/2009/jun/22/ray-bradbury-defends-libraries.

5. "Henry David Thoreau Quotes," BrainyQuote, accessed April 25, 2023, https://www.brainyquote.com/authors/henry-david-thoreau-quotes.

6. John Taylor Gatto, "Nobody Can Educate You Except Yourself—John Taylor Gatto," Bit Chute (video), May 3, 2022, https://www.bitchute.com/video/RNsMHQZyt9S8.

7. Peter Gray, *The Harm of Coercive Schooling* (Cambridge, MA: Tipping Points Press, 2020), 58.

8. "Maria Montessori Quotes," Goodreads, accessed April 25, 2023, https://www.goodreads.com/author/quotes/34106.Maria_Montessori.

9. Payne, Llosa, and Lancaster, *Beyond Winning*, 47.

10. Acuff, *Your New Playlist*, 143.

11. Maria Augusta Trapp, *The Story of the Trapp Family Singers* (New York: William Morrow Paperbacks, 2001), 273.

Chapter 9 The Dynamic Duo

1. "John Holt Quotes," Sandra Dodd (website), accessed April 26, 2023, https://sandradodd.com/holt/quotes.

2. Carla Hannaford, *Smart Moves: Why Learning Is Not All in Your Head* (Salt Lake City: Great River Books, 2005), 26.

3. "More Evidence That Intelligence Is Largely Inherited: Researchers Find That Genes Determine Brain's Processing Speed," Science Daily, March 18, 2009, https://www.sciencedaily.com/releases/2009/03/090317 142841.htm.

4. Hannaford, *Smart Moves*, 27.

5. Levine, *Ready or Not*, 23.

6. "Jimmy Chin Teaches Adventure Photography," MasterClass, accessed April 26, 2023, https://www.masterclass.com/classes/jimmy-chin -teaches-adventure-photography#details.

About the Author

Ginny Yurich is a Michigan homeschooling mother of five and the founder and CEO of 1000 Hours Outside, a global movement, media company, and lifestyle brand intensely focused on bringing back balance between virtual life and real life. She is the host and producer of the extremely popular *The 1000 Hours Outside Podcast*, a keynote public speaker, and a zinnia enthusiast.

Holding a master's degree in education from the University of Michigan, Ginny has been married to her husband, Josh, for over twenty years, and they are lifelong Michiganders. They love raising their five children in the Great Lakes State.

1000 HOURS OUTSIDE

CONNECT with GINNY YURICH:

1000HoursOutside.com   @1000HoursOutside

 @1000HoursOutside   @1000HoursOutside

Low-tide beach walks The Piper Family, Massachusetts • **Making a wand with sticks** The Rarity Family, Scotland • **Making colored ice sculptures** The Baby Bear Family, British Columbia, Canada • **Making a snow volcano** The Cram Family, Missouri • **Making a tape nature catcher** The Thompsons, Wisconsin • **Making an ice rink** The Andersons, Michigan • **Making animal art from leaves** The Ferriolo Family, Nevada • **Making big splashes with rocks** The Byington Family, Missouri • **Making birdseed ornaments** The Wenzel Family, New Jersey • **Making colorful/creative ice ornaments** The Stevens Family, Connecticut • **Making colorful ice globes** The Peers Family, Ontario, Canada • **Making fairy houses together** The Dorzoks, Colorado • **Making flower crowns** The Jinjika Family, Canada • **Making food-coloring ice spheres** Loheac-Whitwood Family, New York • **Making frozen bubbles** The Monzo Tsai Family, New Hampshire • **Making ice ornaments** The Jeziorski Family, Ontario, Canada • **Making magic potion with nature** The Walls, Missouri • **Making memories building our tree house** The Beanes, Texas • **Making mud soup** The Billin Family, Michigan • **Making music and singing hymns** The Hunter Family, Texas • **Making nature bracelets** The Budge Family, New Mexico • **Making nature crafts** The Wilson Family, Virginia • **Making nature pictures on hikes** Team Buhler, Manitoba, Canada • **Making neighborhood friends** The Howalds, Arizona • **Making pigment paints from nature** The Siporin Family, Pennsylvania • **Making rainbows with fall leaves** The Tobelmanns, Michigan • **Making seed bombs in spring** The Girls, California • **Making slime in the shade** The Phares Family, North Carolina • **Making snow angels** The Suhr Family, Idaho • **Making snow palaces in candlelight** The Scotty Clan, Scotland • **Making stuffed animal habitats/zoos** The Gower-Anthony Family, Ontario, Canada • **Making Swedish snölyktar for winter** The McGeehin Family, Michigan • **Manatee watching at Blue Springs** The Skizinski Family, Florida • **Marco Polo on our trampoline** The Pryear Family, Ohio • **Maumee River sunset boat rides** The Gillette Family, Ohio • **Monthly camping trips with friends** The Reeves Family, Tennessee • **Morning snuggles on the porch** The Kitchell Family, Indiana • **Mt. Taylor—four seasons of exploring** The Gudesmith Family, New Mexico • **Mushroom foraging and bird identification** Small Feet Big Adventures, Wales • **Mushroom picking in autumn** The Caldas Schmoi Family, Brazil and Germany • **Music in the park shows** The Allens, Minnesota • **Neighborhood walks in all seasons** The Zimmer Family, Ontario, Canada • **Noticing details in God's handiwork** The Bayer Family, Michigan • **Observing wildlife and gardening** The Wideners, Kentucky • **Our Chesapeake Bay year round** Little Bugs Nature Preschool, Maryland • **Our family loves rain walks** The Woolmans, Washington • **Outdoor ice-skating at Christmas** The Porter Family, West Virginia • **Outdoor movie nights** The Demoret Family, Indiana • **Paddleboarding the North Saskatchewan** The Christian Family, Alberta, Canada • **Paddling and kayaking the PNW** The Pederson Family, Oregon • **Painting in the forest** Katie of Wildflowers Tiney Home Nursery, England • **Painting pine cones** The Sahota Fam, British Columbia, Canada • **Painting snow with food coloring** The Torello-Korpi Family, Utah • **Painting with leaves and sticks** The Baker Farm, Vermont • **Photographing bears in Cades Cove, TN** D & L Martin, Michigan • **Picking and eating cloud candy** The Sekalias Family, Wisconsin • **Picking apples from our tree** The Bushey Family, Vermont • **Picking apples on our farm** The Jaswell Family, Rhode Island • **Picking blackberries** The Riley-Garvins, England • **Picking flowers for the dinner table** The Smit Family, Saskatchewan, Canada • **Picking fruit in the orchard** The Kamps Family, Ontario, Canada • **Picking up rocks along Lake Superior** The Cross Crew, Michigan • **Picking up pine cones after it rains** The Abukaraki Family, Jordan • **Picnic and board games in the park** The Greenmans, Peru • **Picnicking in the woods** The Curetons, Michigan • **Pine cone hunting** The Young Family, California • **Piper's Creek annual salmon runs** Creative Kids, Seattle • **Planting our wildflower garden** The Veltema Family, Michigan • **Playing in the mountain creeks** The Myers Family, Colorado • **Playing I spy on nature walks** The Harris Fam, Florida • **Playing and raking fall leaves** The 147 Gang, Québec, Canada • **Playing at the sandbar** The Schmitts, New York • **Playing baseball in the backyard** The Tubville Family, Tennessee • **Playing catch in the backyard** The Asjes, Kansas • **Playing disc golf together** The McKee Family, Tennessee • **Playing ghost in the graveyard** The Simaikas, Michigan • **Playing in local creeks** The Ames, New Jersey • **Playing in snow at sunrise** The Wilhelms, Ohio • **Playing in the fall leaves** The Kyle Family, New Zealand • **Playing in the rain barefoot** Atikah, Hana & Iman, Singapore • **Playing in the woods** The Peasleys, Ontario, Canada • **Playing on a log** The Bees, Hampshire, England • **Playing on our backyard swing set** The Landuyt Family, Tennessee •

Playing outside games together The Ward Family, Tennessee • **Playing outside with our dogs** The Gunn Family, Prince Edward Island, Canada • **Playing pickleball at the park** The Guntly Family, Illinois • **Playing pickleball in the driveway** The Coetsee Family, South Carolina • **Playing Poohsticks** The North Family, Leicestershire, England • **Playing tag in the backyard** The Avarells, Utah • **Playing tourist in our town** The Moore Family, Georgia • **Puddles in the Hoh Rainforest** The Lee Family, Washington • **Pumpkin farm with the grands** The Hicks Family, Georgia • **Pumpkin picking in autumn** The Roberts, England • **Pumpkin smashing after Halloween** The Spencer Family, Indiana • **Putting our feet in the flowing river** The Arroyo-Sucar Family, Mexico • **Racing sailboats in rainwater runoff** The Fordinals, Texas • **Rainbow brick igloo building** The Block Family, Michigan • **Rainbow hunts while hiking** The Coryell Family, Colorado • **Raking leaves as a family** The Browns, Maryland • **Read-aloud park picnics** The Rodrigues Family, New York • **Reading books right after sunrise** The Turks, Texas • **Reading in the sunshine** The Olivers, Maine • **Reading under a tree** R, L & C Sargent, Alabama • **Reef fishing at Hā'ena, Kaua'i** The Rice Ohana, Hawaii • **Riding bikes around our town** The Diffenderfer Family, Ohio • **Riding bikes to the woods** The Fläscher Family, Germany • **Riding drift bikes together** The Smith Family, Florida • **Riding our horses at sunset** The Hasty Family, Tennessee • **Riding scooters at the arboretum** The Hoffman Family, California • **Roasting apples over a fire** The Muscats, Illinois • **Rock hopping at the creek** The Pelham Family, Delaware • **Rock pooling in Wales** The Sabatier Family, Dunstable, England • **Rolling down big hills** The Gilliams, Virginia • **Rucking South Carolina state parks** The Dover Family, South Carolina • **Running along the Erie Canal** The Hoffman Family, New York • **Running around at the playground** The Boyd Family, North Carolina • **Running barefoot in the rain** The Bonilla Family, Wisconsin • **Running with our goats** The Nytkos, Oklahoma • **Running with the jogging stroller** The Callahan Family, Missouri • **Scat and Tweedle Family, Georgia • **Running/rolling down sand dunes** The Pearsons, Michigan • **S'mores and spooky stories around the campfire** The Callahan Family, Missouri • **Scat and track hunting** Halfway Hippie Homestead, Minnesota • **Scavenger hunt walks in neighborhood** The Minihanes, Rhode Island • **Scooter walk in the neighborhood** The Stroscheins, Illinois • **Scootering through the neighborhood** The Crespo Family, Florida • **Scootering to Teal Lake Park** The Nelsons, Minnesota • **Searching for each season's treasures** The Tupie Family, Pennsylvania • **Searching for fabulous forest fungi** The Parsons, England • **Searching for hiding animals—camouflage** The Greene Family, Minnesota • **Searching for lizards** The Pasillas Family, California • **Secret hideouts are future memories** The Maddox Family, Idaho • **Shark tooth treasure hunt** The Lewis Family, South Carolina • **Shark tooth hunting at beach** The Murphy Family, South Carolina • **Shredding trails on our bikes** The Hogan Family, Georgia • **Sidewalk jumping in the suburbs** The Kendrick Family, New York • **Singing around the campfire** The Johnson Family of Utica, Pennsylvania • **Singing "The Doxology" while hiking** The Sweeney Family, Ohio • **Sitting by the fire** The Lipnick Family, Ohio • **Skate parks, playgrounds, and sand pits** The Heta Whānau, New Zealand • **Skate skiing in the Cascades** The Schorns, Washington • **Skipping rocks at the creek** The Sticklers, Missouri • **Sledding by lantern light** The MacMaster Family, Washington • **Sledding down snowy hills** The Morse Family, Michigan • **Sleeping in the forest** The Moore Family, Ontario, Canada • **Sleeping under the stars** The Murphys, Minnesota • **Sliding down sand dunes on bodyboards** Melina's Family, Australia • **Snorkeling and scuba diving together** The Island Harveys, Bahamas • **Snorkeling coral reefs in Hawaii** The Hills, Hawaii • **Snow ice cream in winter** Team Cary, Oregon • **Snow-tubing down the hill** The Kern Family, Michigan • **Snowshoeing in the Cascade Mountains** The Campbell Family, Oregon • **Snowshoeing in the Keweenaw Peninsula** The Krautheim Family, Michigan • **Snowy picnics with hot soup** The Meinke Family, Michigan • **Snowy walks for Christmas lights** The Achesons, Ontario, Canada • **Soccer at the beach** The Vega Fam, Florida • **Solo backpacking with small kids** The Reeds, Missouri • **Soup lunches outdoors in winter** The Rainbow Cat Family, Bucks, England • **Spelunking in desert mud caves** The Foxes, California • **Splashing at the beach** The 5 Knights, Wales • **Splashing in muddy puddles** The Horton Family, Yorkshire, England • **Splish-splashing in rain puddles** Shawn, Rebekah, Lucas & Nathan, Virginia • **Spring-hopping** The Kays, Florida • **Sprinkler play in our backyard** The Dahtler Family, Australia • **Staying out all day long** Lloyd & Her Boys, England • **Storm watching from the shoreline** The Oriah Family, British Columbia, Canada • **Story time on a blanket** The Cartin Family, Utah • **Storytelling under the stars**